D1592504

A YEAR WITH MARY

JOHN PAUL II

A YEAR
WITH MARY

Daily Meditations

CATHOLIC BOOK PUBLISHING CO.
New York

IMPRIMATUR: ✠ Joseph T. O'Keefe, D.D.
       Vicar General, Archdiocese of New York

This book was originally published in Italian by Edizioni
Piemme, Casale Monferrato, Italy, under the title, *Un
Anno con Maria*. The English translation is by Anthony
M. Buono.

(T-332)

POPE JOHN PAUL II INVITES US TO PRAY WITH MARY

VERY early Karol Wojtyla prayed to the Mother of Christ at Czestochowa, the great place of pilgrimage in Poland where Christians meditate on Mary's accessibility at Cana.

Today the Pope makes a Marian stop on each of his numerous trips. He marks the feasts of Mary by speaking to pilgrims at St. Peter's Square; this pilgrim of Mary prays to the Virgin with an unflagging fervor. In his messages as in his poems we hear the echo of an ardent prayer.

Month after month, the Pope develops a beautiful reflection on Mary and her place in the history of God and human beings.

He bases his thought on the living sources of Bible and Liturgy. And he thus provides beautiful meditation texts that can guide believers' prayer to the Virgin.

Conscious of his responsibility for strengthening the faith of his brothers and sisters, John Paul II contemplates Mary's countenance: she is the Mother of Christ and Mother of human beings, servant of the Lord and associate in His work for the salvation of humankind, the first among believers and redeemed, the teacher of believers on the way to the third millennium in the company of the Church that dispenses the Eucharistic Bread while awaiting the Redeemer of all. The Pope shows how the Church lives day after day from the mystery of Mary, fulfillment of the Paschal Mystery and accomplishment of salvation.

These daily meditations develop the essential mysteries of the Christian faith: from the creation to the redemption, from the resurrection to the effusion of the Spirit, in the expectation of the ultimate encounter of Church and world with the Lord.

While extending an invitation to spend the whole liturgical year with Mary, John Paul II shows himself to be particularly sensitive to the tribulations of human existence.

An ideal companion, this book of Marian prayer will enable readers to rediscover day after day the profound and endless mystery of Mary, Mother of Christ and Mother of all human beings.

CONTENTS

SEASON OF ADVENT

Expectation of the Virgin Mary

SEASON OF CHRISTMAS

Mother of Christ

Servant of the Lord

SEASON OF LENT

Collaboration with God

At the Foot of the Cross

SEASON OF ADVENT

EXPECTATION OF THE VIRGIN MARY

MOTHER OF INDIVIDUALS AND PEOPLES

O Mother of individuals and peoples,
 you know all their sufferings
and their hopes;
you perceive—as a true mother—
all the struggles between good and evil,
between light and darkness,
that trouble the world.
Hear the cry
that we address directly to your heart,
in the Holy Spirit,
and inflame
with all your love of a Mother
and Servant of the Lord
the peoples who most expect your embrace
as well as the peoples whom you more especially
   expect
to trust in you.
Take under your maternal protection
the entire human race
that in a transport of love, O Mother,
we entrust to you.
May there draw near for all
the time
of peace and freedom,
the time
of truth,
of justice, and of hope.

O Mary,
by reason of the mystery of your singular holiness,
    exempt from all stain
from the moment of your conception,
you experience in a particularly profound way
that "all creation groans and is in agony . . .
in the sorrows of childbirth" (Rm 8:22),
"subject as it is to vanity,"
yet "not without hope,
because the world itself will be freed
from its slavery to corruption" (Rm 8:20-21).
We ask you
to cooperate without ceasing
in the "revelation of the sons of God"
that "the created world
eagerly awaits" (Rm 8:19)
so that it too will enter
into the freedom of their joy (cf. Rm 8:21).

WHEN WAS MARY BORN?

MANY ask themselves: "When was our Lady born?" "When did she come into the world?"

They ask this question especially in these times when the second millennium of Christ's birth is approaching. The birth of the Mother must obviously precede the birth of the Son.

Therefore, should we not first celebrate the second millennium of Mary's birth? The Church refers to history and historical dates when she celebrates anniversaries and jubilees, basing herself on precise dates provided by science. Nevertheless, the right rhythm of anniversary and jubilees is determined by "the history of salvation."

We must above all refer in time to the events that have brought us salvation, rather than merely observe—with historical precision—the moment of these events.

MOTHER OF THE CHURCH

THIS title enables us to penetrate the whole mystery of Mary from the instant of her immaculate Conception through the Annunciation, the Visitation, and the Birth of Christ at Bethlehem, and on to Calvary.

It enables all of us to find ourselves "in the Upper Room" where the Apostles with Mary, Mother of Jesus, are assiduous in prayer, awaiting—after the Lord's Ascension—the fulfillment of the promise, that is, the coming of the Holy Spirit, so that the Church may be born!

In the birth of the Church, the one to whom we owe the birth of Christ participates in a particular way.

CALLED CHILDREN OF GOD

THE Church, born once in the Upper Room ("cenacle") of Pentecost, continues to be born in every "cenacle" of prayer. She is born to become "our spiritual Mother in the likeness of the Mother" of the eternal Word. She is born to reveal the characteristics and the strength of that motherhood—the motherhood of the Mother of God—thanks to which we can be called "children of God, for such we are" (1 Jn 3:1).

Indeed, the most holy Fatherhood of God, in the economy of salvation, made use of the virginal motherhood of His "humble servant," to accomplish in the children of the human race the work of the Divine Author.

MARY KEPT ALL THESE THINGS IN HER HEART

BEHOLD Mary the Virgin, Mary the Mother of Christ, whom the Evangelist described as "[keeping] all these things in her heart" (Lk 2:51). She also dwelt upon all the events that comprised the years of her Son's life, in particular those passed in the hidden life at Nazareth.

She is the special witness of the Word Incarnate! She is—like every mother—the living and life-giving Memory of her Son!

She remains in the Church and is present in her in a maternal way, as the latest Council expressed it, and she continues unceasingly to reserve in her heart all that the Church, Mystical Body of her Son, lives and all that—in the Church—the whole human family lives as well as every person redeemed by Christ.

THE FIRST AMONG THE REDEEMED

O IMMACULATE One!
Mother of God and human beings!
We come to you
to venerate the stupendous work
that the Holy Spirit has accomplished in you,
in the generation of Christ,
Redeemer of the world and your Son.
We thank God for you,
the first among the redeemed,
for you who were preserved—
out of all the children of Adam—
from original sin.

O Mary,
"be the Mother of our deliverance from all evil,"
from the evil that weighs on the human conscience
and from the evil that ever more threateningly
darkens the horizon of our century.
You are the light of the first "Advent!"
You are the Morning Star
that precedes the coming of the Messiah.
Be for us "the light"
of this new Advent,
be this Morning Star,
so that the darkness will not engulf us!

DARKNESS FALLS ON HUMAN SOULS

V ERY menacing clouds
accumulate on the horizon of all humankind

and darkness falls on human souls.
Intervene, O Mary, and speak
with your persuasive mother's voice
to the hearts of those
who decide the fates of peoples,
that through dialogue
they may find the ways
for honorable and just compromises
in the differences that keep them apart.
Convince those who bear arms
in the various parts of the world
to accept the invocations of peace
that rise up to them
from martyred and defenseless populations.
Revive, O Mary, in the hearts of all
the sense of human solidarity
toward those
who, deprived of essential goods, are dying of
  hunger;
those who, refugees from their country,
seek refuge for self and family;
those who, lacking a profession,
see their proper domains perilously threatened.
Protect, O Mary, the candor of innocence
in today's children,
who will be the adults of the future.
In your Immaculate Conception,
you reflect with special radiance
the light that has come into the world:
Christ the Lord.
May this "Light lead us toward the future!"

Mirror of justice!
Queen and Mother of peace!

MARY, SIGN OF HOPE

I N the eternal plan of God, Mary was chosen to be
inserted into the world of the Incarnation and the
Redemption. This plan of God was realized through
her free decision made in obedience to the divine
will.

By her "yes," a "yes" that is based on and reflected in all history, she consented to be the Virgin
Mother of our Savior God, the Servant of the Lord,
and at the same time Mother of all the faithful who
in the course of the centuries have become the
brothers and sisters of her Son.

Thanks to her, the Sun of Justice was able to
shine in the world. Thanks to her, the great Savior
of humankind, the reconciler of hearts and consciences, her Son, the God-Man, Jesus Christ, has
come to transform the human condition and,
through His Death and Resurrection, to lift up the
whole human family.

A SIGN OF CONTRADICTION

L IKE a great sign appearing in the heavens in the
fullness of time, the woman dominates all history in her capacity as Virgin Mother of the Son and
Spouse of the Holy Spirit as the servant of humankind.

Thus this woman, associated with the Son, becomes a sign of contradiction for the world and at the same time a sign of hope that all generations shall call Blessed.

This woman conceived spiritually before conceiving physically; this woman accepted the Word of God; this woman was intimately and irrevocably inserted into the mystery of the Church, exercising a spiritual motherhood in regards to all peoples.

The woman is honored as the Queen of Apostles, even without being inserted into the hierarchical constitution of the Church. And it is precisely this woman who has made possible the whole hierarchy, placing into the world the Shepherd and Bishop of our souls.

THE ANGEL WAS SENT TO A TOWN CALLED NAZARETH

"THE Angel Gabriel was sent from God to a town of Galilee called Nazareth" (Lk 1:26). Gabriel was sent by God to Mary of Nazareth to announce to her—and in her to the whole human race—the mission of the Word. Behold, God wants to send the eternal Son so that by becoming man He can grant human beings Divine life, Divine filiation, grace, and truth.

The mission of the Son begins precisely at this moment at Nazareth when Mary hears the words pronounced by Gabriel: "You have found grace

with God. Behold, you shall conceive and bear a
Son, and you shall give him the Name Jesus" (Lk
1:30-31).

THE POWER OF THE MOST HIGH
WILL OVERSHADOW YOU

THE mission of this Son, the eternal Word, begins
when Mary of Nazareth, a virgin "betrothed
to a man named Joseph, of the house of David"
(Lk 1:27), hearing the words of Gabriel, replies:
"Behold, I am the servant of the Lord. Let it be
done to me as you say" (Lk 1:38).

At that moment the mission of the Son on earth
begins.

The word of the same substance as the Father becomes flesh in the womb of the Virgin. The Virgin
herself cannot comprehend how all this will be
realized.

Indeed, before replying: "Let it be done to me,"
she asks: "How shall this happen since I do not
know man?" (Lk 1:34).

And she receives the decisive response: "The Holy
Spirit will come upon you and the power of the Most
High will overshadow you; hence the holy Offspring
to be born will be called Son of God . . . nothing is
impossible with God" (Lk 1:35-37).

THE MISSION OF THE SON BEGINS

FROM this moment Mary understands. She asks no other question. She simply says: "Let it be done to me as you say" (Lk 1:38). And the Word becomes flesh (cf. Jn 1:14). The Mission of the Son in the Holy Spirit begins. "The mission of the Son and the mission of the Holy Spirit" begin. At this first stage the mission is directed to her alone, to the Virgin of Nazareth.

The Holy Spirit comes upon her, first. In her human and virginal substance, Mary is overshadowed by the power of the Most High. Thanks to this power and as a consequence of the Holy Spirit, she remains a Virgin.

The mission of the Son initiates in her, under her heart. The mission of the Holy Spirit, "who proceeds from the Father and from the Son" also reaches her first, the soul who is His most pure and most sensible Spouse.

"FULL OF GRACE"

"FULL of grace . . ." (Lk 1:28): when these words were pronounced, "the Advent that humankind was awaiting" reached its summit.

That is why the Immaculate Conception of the Blessed Virgin Mary each year finds its liturgical place during the season of Advent.

Indeed, this greeting "full of grace" testifies to the mystery of the "Immaculate Conception." This greeting of the Archangel prepares for the revelation of the Divine Motherhood of Mary.

"You shall conceive and bear a Son, and you shall give Him the Name Jesus. . . . The Holy Spirit will come upon you and the power of the Most High will overshadow you; hence the holy Offspring to be born will be called Son of God" (Lk 1:31, 35).

THE IMMACULATE CONCEPTION

MARY! "You have found grace with God" (Lk 1:30). You are "full of grace."

The fullness of grace signifies the Divine Motherhood. The fullness of grace thus signifies the Immaculate Conception.

The Immaculate Conception is in "view of the Divine Motherhood." Such is the order of grace, that is, the salvific economy of God.

On the solemnity the Church prays in the following words:

"O God, by the Immaculate Conception of the Virgin You have prepared a worthy dwelling for Your Son and in the prevision of her death preserved her from every stain of sin. Grant us also by her intercession to come to meet You in holiness and purity of spirit. We ask this through Christ our Lord. . . ."

REDEEMED IN AN EXCEPTIONAL WAY

THE liturgical prayer to Mary Immaculate contains all the elements of the "faith of the Church" preserved in Tradition and proclaimed as a dogma by the Servant of God Pope Pius IX in 1854.

In the first place, the preservation from original sin, that is, Mary's Immaculate Conception, was to prepare "a worthy dwelling" for the Son of God in the Incarnation.

Secondly, this exemption from sin, that is, the Immaculate Conception, is a privilege that the Mother of God owes to the Redemption worked by the Cross of Christ.

Thus, the mystery of the Immaculate Conception of the Virgin Mary leads us "to Bethlehem and at the same time to Calvary." In a certain sense it guides us first to Calvary and then to Bethlehem.

Mary was "redeemed in a special way" in the first instant of her conception, in prevision of the Sacrifice of Christ the Redeemer on Calvary so that she could become the Mother of the Redeemer at Nazareth and in Bethlehem.

THE BEGINNING
OF THE FULLNESS OF TIME

THE Immaculate Conception" is both the sign and the announcement of the New Time," It is the beginning of the fullness of times about which

Paul the Apostle speaks. It shines forth not only on the horizon of the first Advent, which was already accomplished on the night of the earthly Birth of God, but also "on the horizon of the definitive Advent," to which humankind is continually drawing closer without knowing either "the day or the hour" (Mt 25:13).

In the Liturgy of the Hours, St. Anselm speaks of the latter Advent with truly inspired words: "God is the Father of created realities, and Mary is 'the Mother of uncreated realities.' God is the Father of created realities, and Mary is 'the Mother of uncreated realities.' God is the Father of the constitution of all things, and Mary is the 'Mother of the reconstitution of all things.' "

The Immaculate Conception has given birth to the work of the "renewal of the human race" oppressed by the heritage of the first Adam.

CHOSEN BY GOD'S SALVIFIC PLAN

IN the solemnity of the Immaculate Conception we confess that Mary—chosen in a special way and eternally by God in His loving salvific plan—has also experienced salvation in a special way. In an exceptional manner she has been redeemed by the work of the One to Whom as a Virgin Mother she was to transmit human life.

The readings of the Liturgy also speak of this. St. Paul in the Epistle to the Ephesians writes: "Blessed be the God and Father of our Lord Jesus Christ,

Who blessed us with every spiritual blessing on high in Christ.

"God chose us in Him before the world began, to be holy and blameless in His sight, in love" (Eph 1:3-4).

CHOSEN BEFORE THE WORLD BEGAN

THESE words "refer" in a particular and exceptional manner to "Mary." Indeed, she—more than all other human beings and more than the Angels—"has been chosen in Christ before the world began," because in a unique manner and one that could not be repeated she was chosen "for Christ" and predestined to be His Mother.

Then completing this idea in his Epistle to the Ephesians, Paul goes on: "He predestined us through Christ Jesus to be His adopted children.

"Such was His will and pleasure that all might praise the glorious grace He has freely given us in His Beloved" (Eph 1:5-6).

DIVINE ADOPTION

INSOFAR as these words refer to all Christians, they also refer to Mary in an exceptional way. Precisely in her role as Mother she acquired "the Divine adoption" to the highest degree; chosen to be an adopted daughter in the eternal Son of God precisely because, in the Divine economy of salvation, He was to become her true Son, born of her, and thus Son of Man, and she—as we frequently chant—Beloved Daughter of the Father!

And finally, the Apostle writes: "In Him, that is, in Christ we were chosen; for in the decree of God, Who administers everything according to His will and counsel, we were predestined to praise His glory by being the first to hope in Christ" (Eph 1:11-12).

GRACE-LADEN

NO one "has hoped" more fully, more absolutely, and more deeply in Christ than His Mother Mary.

Neither has anyone more than Mary "been made an heir in Him," in Christ! No one in the history of the world was more Christocentric, more Christ-bearing, than she and no one was more like Him, not merely by the natural likeness of the Mother with her Son but also by the likeness of the Spirit and of holiness.

And since no one more than she existed in conformity with the plan of the will of God, no one more than she in this world existed "to the praise of His glory"—because no one existed in Christ and through Christ more than the Woman through whom Christ was born on earth.

This is the praise of the Immaculate Conception that the Liturgy proclaims in the words of the Epistle to the Ephesians.

And all this richness of Paul's theology can be found enclosed in these words of Luke: "Full of grace" (kecharitomene").

A PARTICULAR MYSTERY OF THE FAITH

THE Immaculate Conception is a particular mystery of the faith—and it is also a particular solemnity. It is the feast of Advent par excellence.

This feast—and even this mystery—makes us think of the "beginning" of human beings on earth, their original innocence, their lost grace and original sin.

This is why we read first of all the passage from the Book of Genesis that gives the image of this "origin."

When we read in this text of the woman whose posterity "will crush the head of the serpent" (cf Gn 3:15), we see "in this woman," in accord with Tradition, "Mary" presented precisely immaculate by the working of the Son of God, to Whom she was to give human nature.

"I AM THE SERVANT OF THE LORD"

WE cannot find it surprising that at the beginning of human history, understood as the history of salvation, Mary is also inscribed. For—as we have read in St. Paul—before the creation of the world every Christian has been chosen in Christ and for Christ: and this holds even more for Mary!

The Immaculate Conception is thus a particular, exceptional, and unique work of God: "full of grace. . . ."

When, at the time appointed by the Holy Trinity, the Angel came to Mary and said: "Do not be afraid. . . . You shall conceive and bear a Son, and you shall give Him the Name Jesus. He will be great and will be called Son of the Most High" (Lk 1:30-32), only she who was "full of grace" could respond as Mary did: "Behold, I am the servant of the Lord. Let it be done to me as you say" (Lk 1:38).

TEMPLE OF THE SPIRIT

VIEWED in God's eternal plan for human beings, Mary is closely united to the Incarnate Word by an indissoluble bond of motherhood and from all eternity is associated with His redemptive work. Because of this mission of hers, it was fitting that there not be in her any stain of original sin from the first instant of her existence.

In the history of human generations her immaculate conception represents the most perfect realization of the gratuitous action of the Holy Spirit Who molds her and renders her a new creature, an uncontaminated land, a temple of the Spirit, from the first instant.

Viewed in the history and modality of the Redemption, the Immaculate Conception of Mary signifies not only the first person redeemed, hence the dawn of the Redemption, but also this point: while for all the rest of the human race redemption means "liberation" from the sin imputed, for Mary who like every other human being is in need of redemption it means "preservation" from original sin itself, from the first instant of her life in virtue of the merits of Christ, the sole and universal Redeemer.

"HE HAS DONE GREAT THINGS FOR ME"

"MY soul proclaims the greatness of the Lord,
my spirit rejoices in God my Savior,
for He has looked upon His servant in her lowliness;
all ages to come shall call me blessed.
God Who is mighty has done great things for me" (Lk 1:46-49).

"God Who is mighty has done great things for me," exclaims she who at the Annunciation has called herself "servant" and who in this "Magnificat" describes herself in an analogous way: "He has looked upon His servant in her lowliness."

Oh! how greatly we love this "servant of the Lord"! How deeply we entrust to her everything and everyone, Church and the world! How much this "lowliness" of hers tells us! It constitutes as it were the adequate space for God to reveal Himself; for

God to be born of her; for God to work through her "from generation to generation."

"The words of Mary" are truly "full of Advent!" It is difficult to "feel" more keenly the approach of God if we do not heed these words!

ENCOUNTER WITH THE LIVING GOD

"**G**OD Who is mighty has done great things for me, and holy is His Name" (Lk 1:49).

The words pronounced in the course of a visit to Elizabeth fully express what the Virgin of Nazareth is experiencing in her heart after the Annunciation.

Adoration of God filled with joy and joy filled with adoration of God: such is the state of her blessed soul, such are the deepest sentiments that her heart nourishes.

They manifest themselves above all in the words of the "Magnificat."

In the "Magnificat" there springs forth "that gratitude filled with humility" which is the infallible sign of an encounter with the living God. Mary responds to the "gift from on high" not only by her words but also by the whole silence of the mystery of Advent that is realized in her.

THE ADVENT OF HUMANITY

MARY is the one in whom "the Advent of all humanity" has assumed its fullest form: in her it has attained its "zenith."

However, this "zenith" of humankind continues in its completion and reaches its fullness in the Church. A pilgrim on earth and like an "exile" searching for the things from on high, the Church experiences the Lord's coming "until the day when with the Bridegroom she will appear clothed in glory" (cf. LG 6); and the Advent lived by the Church is the sacrament or sign and instrument of union with God.

Every day in her Liturgy the Church chants the "Magnificat" together with our Lady. In this way, the Advent completed in the Mother of God is "prolonged" throughout all the days in the life of the Church.

THE BEAUTY OF MARY

IN order to speak of Mary, of that Beauty which is fully known only by God, but which at the same time speaks so tellingly to human beings, we wish to make use of the words of two of the greatest Fathers and writers of the Church "of the East and the West."

Commenting on a verse of Psalm 86, St. Germanus of Constantinople declares: "Inspired by the Spirit, holy David sings of you: 'Marvelous things are said of you, O city of God.'

"In mentioning so clearly the city of the great King, about which marvelous things are said, David without any doubt is speaking of the one who was truly chosen and is raised above everyone else not by taller houses or by higher hills but by the fact that she far excells all others in the splendor of magnificent Divine virtues, by her extraordinary purity.

"[David] is speaking of Mary, the most chaste and most immaculate Mother of God, in whom dwells the One Who is truly the King of kings and Lord of lords, or better, the One in Whom the fullness of the Divinity corporally dwells" (Hom 9; PG:372).

MARY REDEEMED IN ADVANCE

ST. Ambrose, the great Bishop of Milan, presents Mary to us as the one "redeemed in advance" by Christ her Son: "She is truly the blessed Mary because she was superior to the priest Zechariah. Whereas Zechariah had refused to believe, she corrected this error.

"It should not surprise us that the Lord, wishing to redeem the world, began His work with Mary. If by means of her the salvation of all humans was being proposed, she had to be the first to receive 'the fruit of salvation' from her Son."

THE BEAUTY OF GRACE

I HAVE wished in a special way to combine these two voices because in them the two traditions of East and West speak, united in the veneration of this Beauty that God Himself has prepared "at the beginning of the mystery of the Incarnation."

We are going to repeat the words with which the Archangel Gabriel greeted Mary at the moment of the Incarnation: "Hail, full of grace" (Lk 1:28). Human beings are sensitive to beauty, not only to the external beauty perceived by the senses but also to the beauty of the spirit.

In the words of the Archangel, pronounced at the moment of the Incarnation, it is by her name that she is called the greatest spiritual beauty, which has its origin in God Himself. And above all He finds His delight in her.

Let us pray that this beauty, the beauty of the grace of God, may never cease to attract human hearts.

"I AM THE IMMACULATE CONCEPTION"

TO St. Bernadette, who had asked for her name several times, the Blessed Virgin said: "I am the Immaculate Conception." By these words she clearly manifested not only that she had been conceived without sin but also that she was the Immaculate Conception in person, in the same way that a white object is one thing and whiteness is another; a perfect object is one thing and perfection is another.

The Immaculate Conception is the name that reveals with precision who Mary is. It not only affirms some quality about her but also defines her person in exact fashion. Mary is profoundly holy in the totality of her existence, from her very beginnings.

IMMACULATE BECAUSE SHE IS MOTHER OF GOD

SUBLIME supernatural greatness was bestowed on Mary because of Jesus Christ; it is in Him and through Him that God granted her a share in the fullness of sanctity. Mary is Immaculate because she is Mother of God, and she becomes Mother of God because she is Immaculate, declares Maximilian Kolbe in concise fashion.

The Immaculate Conception of Mary manifests, in a unique and sublime way, the absolute centrality and universal saving function of Jesus Christ. "From the Divine Maternity flow all the graces accorded to the Blessed Virgin Mary, and the first of them is the Immaculate Conception."

For this reason, Mary is not simply like Eve before sin, but she was enriched with an incomparable fullness of grace because she was to be the Mother of Christ, and the Immaculate Conception was the beginning of a prodigious and undiminished expansion of her supernatural life.

UNION BETWEEN MARY AND THE HOLY SPIRIT

THE mystery of Mary's holiness must be viewed in the totality of the Divine order of salvation so that it may be appreciated in a harmonious way and so that it will not appear as some privilege that separates her from the Church, which is the Body of Christ.

Father Maximilian Kolbe takes great care to associate Mary's Immaculate Conception and her function in the Divine plan of salvation with the mystery of the Trinity and in a special way with the person of the Holy Spirit. With depth and ingenuity he develops the multiple aspects contained in the notion of the "Bride of the Holy Spirit," which is well known in patristic and theological tradition and is suggested by the New Testament: "The Holy Spirit will come upon you and the power of the Most High will overshadow you; hence, the holy Offspring to be born will be called the Son of God" (Lk 1:35).

This is an analogy, stresses St. Maximilian, that enables us to see the ineffable, intimate, and fecund union between the Holy Spirit and Mary.

EVERYWHERE THERE IS LOVE

FATHER Kolbe gazes with admiration at the Divine plan of salvation, which has its source in the Father Who wished to communicate freely to creatures the Divine life of Jesus Christ and which is manifested in Mary Immaculate in a wondrous way. Fascinated and enraptured, he exclaims: "Everywhere there is love"; God's gratuitous love is the response to all the interrogations; "God is love," affirms St. John (1 Jn 4:8).

All that exists is a reflection of the gratuitous love of God, and that is why every creature expresses in some way the infinite splendor of that love. In a particular fashion, love is the center and summit of the human person, made in the image and likeness of God.

Mary Immaculate, the most exalted and most perfect of human persons, reproduces in an eminent way the image of God. She is therefore made capable of loving Him with an incomparable intensity, as the Immaculata without deviation or slackening. She is the unique servant of the Lord (cf. Lk 1:38) who by her free and personal "fiat" ("let it be done") responds to God's love by always doing what He asks of her.

THE SUMMIT OF LOVE

MARY'S response, like that of every other person, is not an autonomous response but a grace and gift of God. In such a response is implicated all her freedom, the freedom of the Immaculata.

"In the union of the Holy Spirit with Mary, love does not bring together only these two persons. The first love is all the love of the Blessed Trinity, while the second, that of Mary, is all the love of creation. Thus, in this union heaven is united with earth, the whole of uncreated Love is united with created love. . . . It is the summit of love" (Maximilian Kolbe).

OUR MOTHER

MARY is the heir and the fulfillment of the faith of Abraham. Just as the Patriarch is regarded as "our father," so Mary must with greater reason be regarded as "our Mother" in faith.

Abraham is at the origin and Mary is at the summit of the generations of Israel. Abraham anticipates and represents before God the people of the promise; Mary, a descendant of Abraham and privileged heir of his faith, obtains the fruit of the promise.

Through Mary's faith and obedience, all the families of the earth are blessed, in accord with the promise made to Abraham (cf. Gn 12:3)

THE SALVATION OF THE WORLD

THE words of the Virgin Mary: "Behold, I am the servant of the Lord. Let it be done to me as you say" (Lk 1:38), evoke not only the figure and attitude of Abraham but also the image of all the servants of the Lord who have collaborated with Him in the History of Salvation. More generally, they recall the words of the children of Israel at the foot of Mt. Sinai on the day of the Covenant: "We will do everything that the Lord has told us" (Ex 24:3).

Mary's response is personal, but it also has a communitary significance. Her "Yes" includes the faith of ancient Israel and gives rise to the faith of the Church.

Mary's adherence to the Lord, through a solidarity of grace, is a blessing for all who believe. Attached to her faith is the salvation of the world.

MARY PRECEDES US IN FAITH, HOPE, AND LOVE

MARY, insofar as she is the Immaculate Conception, bears within herself, more than any other human person, the mystery of those eternal Divine destinies that have come to humans in the beloved Son of God:

—the human destiny "to Grace" and to the holiness of the Divine filiation;

—the human destiny to glory in the God of infinite majesty.

Mary precedes us all in the great procession of faith, hope, and love.

Indeed, as the Second Vatican Council has stated, "in the mystery of the Church, which is justly termed mother and virgin, the Blessed Virgin Mary has 'gone before,' presenting herself in an eminent and singular manner as a Virgin and Mother" (LG 63).

THE DAWN OF ADVENT

MARY illumines the People of God with the Divine light that more fully reflects the light of the Divine Word.

"The Mother of Jesus"—it is still the Council stressing this point—"shines forth on earth before the pilgrim People of God as a sign of sure hope and consolation" (LG 63).

When the light begins to shine through Mary on the "horizon of the history" of humankind—when, with the birth of Mary, there appeared in the world the one who was the Immaculate Conception—then there has begun in the History of Salvation the dawn of the Advent of the Son of God. And then the work of the Redemption has taken on its form determined from all eternity.

IMAGE OF THE CHURCH

THE Conciliar Constitution on the Church, "Lumen Gentium," dedicates its eighth and last chapter to the Virgin Mary, Mother of God.

We can say that in this chapter the Church fixes her gaze in a special manner on the one whom St. Anselm always called the "figure of the Church . . . that is, in the order of faith, love, and perfect union with Christ"(cf. LG 62).

"Indeed, in the mystery of the Church, which is also rightfully called mother and virgin, the Blessed Virgin Mary has gone before, presenting herself in an eminent and singular manner as Virgin and Mother" (LG 63).

HE CREATED HER
THROUGH HIS HOLY SPIRIT

THIS manner of fixing our gaze on Mary finds its expression in the Liturgy and the whole life of the Church. The solemnity of the Immaculate Conception seems to be the moment when the Church's gaze fixed on Mary goes even further, not only to the very "beginning" of her earthly existence but also to the very "beginning" of the history of humankind and the History of Salvation.

Indeed, we can say it goes even further back than that: to the eternal Divine Thought and Love, in which Mary was conceived infinitely before her conception on earth. Following the idea of the Church, we can adapt to the Most Holy Virgin the words of the Book of Sirach: "He has created her through His Holy Spirit . . . and has poured her out upon all His creation" (Sir 1:9ff).

THE FULFILLMENT OF THE TIMES

OUR thought continues to dwell today on the rich meaning of this great event of salvation.

It refers not only to the person of Mary but also to the beginning of the new People of God, that is, the Church of Christ, and to a new humankind that with her becomes the family of God.

Indeed, if we consider Mary in the fullness of her mystery and mission, she expresses her autonomous personality not only at the summit and beginning of the Church but also within the dynamism of the History of Salvation.

She is thus so intimately joined to the Church as to appear as an incarnation and a living image of the mystical personality of the Church herself, Bride of Christ, expressing from the first instant of her existence all the riches of grace that animate her.

Concerning this point, there comes to mind the precious indication of chapter eight of "Lumen Gentium," which, interpreting the intuition of St. Luke, tells us: "With her, the exalted Daughter of Zion, and after a long expectation for the promise, the times are fulfilled and the new dispensation is established."

THE BEGINNING OF THE CHURCH OF CHRIST

PLACED at the point of contact between the Old and the New Covenant, Mary is the end of the Messianic Church of Israel and the beginning of the Church being born of Christ.

It is she who is the ultimate and perfect expression of the old People of God, born of Adam, and the first exalted realization of the new People of God, which is being born of Christ. Hence, with Mary there are concluded the promises, the prefigurations, the prophecies, and the spiritualities of the Old Testament Church, and the New Testament Church, without spot or stain, begins in the fullness of the grace of the Holy Spirit.

This ecclesiological dimension, proclaimed by the Second Vatican Council, is the new itinerary that enables us to read and understand the mystery of Mary in all its extension and profundity.

GOD'S MASTERPIECE

IN the light of the Second Vatican council, the Immaculate Conception of the Mother of God and our Mother takes on a richer and more ecclesial meaning. With her, masterpiece of God the Father and most pure reflection of the grace of the Holy Spirit, the Church of Jesus Christ has begun. In Mary we see the Immaculate Conception of the Church, which is temple and bride without spot or stain.

It is in her that the Church feels it has reached her highest perfection, without shadow of sin; and it is in her—insofar as she is a prototype, sign, and help—that the ecclesial community, still a pilgrim on earth, is inspired, urging itself to advance in holiness and in the struggle against sin.

"THE GATE OF HEAVEN"

"HOLY Mother of our Redeemer" ("Alma Redemptoris Mater") . . . , these words serve as a beginning for the Marian antiphon that the Church recites especially in the Liturgy of Advent as well as in the Liturgy of the Christmas Season.

Portraying in this antiphon the state of humankind after original sin, the Church prays to the one who is "the Gate of heaven" and "Star of the sea" to come to the aid of this humankind and every person who wants to rise again from the fall and attain freedom from the chains of evil: "Assist your people who have fallen yet strive to rise again. To the wonder of nature you bore your Creator."

These words have a penetrating tone. They embody a kind of nostalgia for the good lost and at the same time the hope associated with the Lord's birth.

The one who, through God's supernatural power, has become Mother of the Eternal Word, can help individuals and the whole of humankind.

CHOSEN TO BE THE MOTHER

THE whole visible world has been created for human beings, as the Book of Genesis attests. The beginning of Advent in God is His eternal "plan of creation" of the world and human beings, a plan born out of love. This love is manifested by the eternal "choice of human beings in Christ," the incarnate Word.

Mary is present in this eternal Advent. From among all human beings whom the Father has chosen in Christ, she was chosen in a particular and exceptional manner, because she was chosen in Christ to be the Mother of Christ.

Thus, more than any other human "predestined by the Father" to the dignity of His adopted sons and daughters, Mary has been predestined in a very special way "to the praise and glory of His grace," which the Father "has freely given us" in His beloved Son (cf. Eph 1:6).

MOTHER OF THE ETERNAL WORD

THE sublime glory of her very special grace was to be the "Motherhood" of the Eternal Word. In consideration of this Motherhood, she has also obtained in Christ the grace of the "Immaculate Conception." In this way Mary is inserted in that first eternal Advent of the Word, predisposed by the Father's Love for creation and for human beings.

The "second Advent" has a historical character. It was accomplished in the time between the fall of the first human being and the Coming of the Redeemer.

Today's Liturgy also tells us about this Advent and shows how Mary from the very beginning is inserted in it. Indeed, when the first sin manifested itself, with the unexpected shame of our first parents, then God also revealed for the first time the Redeemer of the world, preannouncing His Mother at the same time.

"I WILL PUT ENMITY BETWEEN YOU AND THE WOMAN"

THE preannouncement of the Mother took place through the words in which Tradition sees the "protoevangelium," that is, the embryo and announcement of the Gospel itself, the Good News.

Here are those words: "I will put enmity between you and the woman, and between your offspring and hers; He will crush your head, while you strike at His heel" (Gn 3:15).

These are mysterious words. Yet, with all their archaic flavor, they reveal the future of humankind and the Church. This future is seen in "terms of a struggle between the Spirit of Darkness," who is "a liar and the father of lies" (Jn 8:44), and the "Son of the Woman," Who will come among human beings as "the way, and the truth, and the life" (Jn 14:6).

THE THIRD ADVENT

MARY is the beginning of the third Advent, because she has given to the world the One Who will accomplish this eternal choice. In accomplishing it, He will make it the culminating fact of the history of humankind.

He will give it the concrete form of the Gospel, the Eucharist, the Word, and the Sacraments. In this way, that eternal choice will penetrate the lives of human souls and the life of this particular community that calls itself Church.

Just as the second Advent takes us close to the one whose Son was "to crush the head of the serpent," so the third Advent does not take us away from her but continually enables us to remain in her presence, close to her.

EXPECTATION OF THE FULFILLMENT OF THE TIMES

THE third Advent is nothing else but the expectation of the definitive fulfillment of the times: it is contemporaneously the time of struggle and opposition, in continuation of the original prevision: "I will put enmity between you and the woman . . ." (Gn 3:15).

The difference consists in the fact that the Woman is already known to us by name. She is the Immaculate Conception. She is known by her virginity and her motherhood. She is the Mother of Christ and of the Church, Mother of God and of human beings: "Mary of our Advent."

"I DO NOT KNOW MAN"

SOLELY by the "infinite power of love" can we explain the fact that the Word of God, God the Son, became man.

Solely by the omnipotence that loves, solely by the inscrutable power of God's love can we explain the fact that the Virgin—daughter of human parents and human generation—becomes the Mother of God.

Yet "even for her," this fact was incomprehensible: "How shall this happen since I do not know man?" (Lk 1:34).

And probably it was difficult to believe on the part "of the people," whose child she was, the people who throughout its history was waiting for just this: the coming of the Messiah, and who saw in this the principal purpose of its vocation, trials, and sufferings.

And this fact is difficult to be grasped by so many people and nations, even if they accept the existence of God, and even if they have recourse to His goodness and mercy.

However, "nothing is impossible with God!"

"THEOTOKOS," MOTHER OF GOD

THIS word resounds with a distant echo: it was pronounced with great transports of faith and love 1550 years ago at the Council of Ephesus, and from that date it has always been solemnly pronounced by the Church: in the Liturgy and the Magisterium [Teaching Office], in the prayers in the language of so many diverse nations and peoples, and contemporaneously with a similar "sense of faith" by the whole people of God.

"Theotokos": "Mother of God."

Let us pronounce this word with special love and veneration.

When we say the words, "The Angel of the Lord announced to Mary, and she conceived of the Holy Spirit," we express the total and full truth contained

.in this term "Theotokos." It is she who at the Word of the Eternal Father transmitted in the Angelic annunciation "conceived," that is, became Mother, of the Eternal Word by the power of the Holy Spirit. In her the Word became flesh.

GOD HAS CHOSEN THE MOTHER

IN His eternal love God has, from all eternity, chosen human beings: He has chosen them in His Son. God has chosen human beings so that they can attain the fullness of the good by sharing in His very life: Divine life through grace. He has chosen them from eternity and irreversibly.

Neither original sin nor the whole history of personal faults and social sins has been able to dissuade the Eternal Father from His plan of love. Nothing has been able to annul the choice He has made of us in the Eternal Son, the Word Who is consubstantial with the Father.

This choice was to take form in the Incarnation and the Son of God was to become Man for our salvation. Precisely because of this the Eternal Father has chosen a Mother for Him from among human beings.

FROM THE LINE OF DAVID

EACH of us became a human being because we are conceived and born from the maternal womb. The Eternal Father has chosen the same route for the humanity of His Eternal Son. He has chosen a Mother for Him from among the people to whom He had for centuries entrusted in a special way His mysteries and His promises.

He chose her from the line of David and at the same time from all humankind. He chose her from royal blood but at the same time from the lowly.

He chose her from the beginning, from the first moment of her conception, rendering her worthy of the Divine Motherhood, to which she was to be called at the appointed time.

He made her the first to inherit the holiness of her Son—the first among those redeemed by His Blood, which He had humanly speaking received from her. He made her immaculate in the very moment of her conception.

THE SIGNS OF THE TIMES

THE signs of the times indicate that we are immersed within the orbit of a great struggle between good and evil, between the affirmation and the denial of God, of His presence in the world, and of the salvation that has its beginning and its end in Him.

Do not these "signs indicate to us the "Woman" in whose company we must journey through the span of time traced out by the century and the millennium that are about to come to a close? Is it not in unison with her that we are to confront the travails with which our century is filled? Is it not in her that we are to find the "strength" and the hope that are born from the very heart of the Gospel?

In accord with the Second Vatican Council, let us meditate on Mary's marvelous presence in the mystery of Christ and of the Church.

"I WILL HEAR WHAT GOD PROCLAIMS"

"**I** WILL heed what God the Lord says:
He proclaims peace
To His people and His faithful ones
    and to those who return wholeheartedly to Him.
His salvation is near to those who fear Him,
    and His glory will dwell in our land" (Ps 85:9f).

Behold, "the virgin of Nazareth" hears what God proclaims to her through the medium of His Messenger: "You shall conceive and bear a Son, and you shall give Him the Name Jesus. . . . The Holy Spirit will come upon you and the power of the Most High will overshadow you; hence, the Holy Offspring to be born will be called the Son of God" (Lk 1:31-35).

ADVENT IS AN ENCOUNTER

THE Virgin of Nazareth hears what God says to her. She listens: "not only does she receive the word," but "she is obedient to the Word" and responds: "Behold, I am the servant of the Lord. Let it be done to me as you say" (Lk 1:38). In this way,

Advent is completed: the first Advent of humankind.

Advent signifies the nearness "of salvation," it signifies "God's glory on earth."

"Advent is an encounter." Psalm 85 speaks of it in this way:

"Kindness and truth shall meet
    justice and peace shall kiss" (Ps 85:11).

Behold, together with the Word Who became flesh in the bosom of the Virgin justice descends. "It comes from God."

It comes as grace and peace: the grace and peace of reconciliation with God in the Eternal Son.

What does this justice offered to humans in Christ require as correspondence? What must human beings bear in their hearts?

"They must bring forth fidelity" because
"Truth shall spring out of the earth
    and justice shall look down from heaven"
    (Ps 85:12).

THE MIRACLE OF THE IMMACULATA

"SING to the Lord a new song,
    for he has done wondrous deeds;
His right hand has won victory for Him,
    His holy arm" (Ps 98:1).

Formerly, the words of this psalm bore witness to the exodus from the slavery of Egypt.

Today they proclaim "the preservation from the slavery of sin." They recount "the miracle of God's grace." This miracle constitutes a greater victory than the victory that the God of Israel carried off against the oppressors of His People.

The miracle of the Immaculate Conception is "the victory of Christ the Redeemer." Sin, which is the heritage of Adam—original sin—is overcome from the first instant of the Conception of the one who has been chosen to be the Mother of the Redeemer.

This miracle of Grace has been worked by the "right hand" and by the "holy arm" of the One Who was nailed to the Cross for the redemption of the sins of all humankind.

THE REVELATION OF THE NEW LIFE

THE one who was eternally chosen to be His Mother "was redeemed in a privileged way!"

This is the sign of the "new Beginning," the revelation of the "new Life" in the innermost depths of the human being.

This is the undeniable "testimony of salvation": God is Savior!

"All the ends of the earth have seen
the salvation of our God" (Ps 98:3).

The Church at Rome—and in all the confines of the earth—intones the chant of the Immaculate Conception. With this chant she proclaims the work of salvation, which through God's will is realized in the history of humankind over the whole earth.

HAIL, HOLY MOTHER OF GOD

HAIL, holy Mother of God,
glorious and blessed Virgin!
Hail, Mother of the Church,
holy Mary: our Mother!
You open your arms to embrace your children!
Small and great—you listen to them and console them;
you show them the source of peace:
Jesus, the fount of your womb.

I present to your Mother's love
men and women [of the world]. . . .

I pray to you for babies and youths:
may they advance in life
guided by faith and hope
that open their hearts
to the invitations of the Lord of the harvest.

I pray to you for persons of the third age:
may they enjoy peace and know how to love one another.

I pray to you for couples:
may they discover the ever-new beauty
of a love that is generous and open to life.

I pray to you for families:
may they live the joy of that unity
in which each gives to the others
the best of oneself.

I pray to you for celibates:
may they discover happiness
in service and in being useful
to their brothers and sisters.

I pray to you for consecrated persons:
may they give testimony,
through their free commitment,
to the call of Christ
for the construction of a new world.

SOURCE OF ALL GRACES

HAIL, O Mother, Queen of the world.
You are the Mother of fair Love,
you are the Mother of Jesus,
and the source of all grace,
the fragrance of all virtue,
the mirror of all purity.

You are joy in weeping,
victory in the struggle,
and hope in death.

How sweet is your name in our mouths,
what delightful harmony in our ears,
what intoxication in our hearts!

You are the happiness of the suffering,
the crown of martyrs,
and the beauty of virgins.

We beg you
to guide us after this our exile
to the possession of your Son Jesus.

HELP US TO ANNOUNCE CHRIST

HELP us, in this great effort we are making to "encounter" in an ever more mature way "our brothers and sisters in the faith," with whom so many things unite us, although there is still something that separates us.

Grant that, through all the means of knowledge, mutual respect, love, and common collaboration in various fields, we may gradually rediscover the Divine plan of that unity into which we must enter and introduce all others, so that the unique sheepfold of Christ may recognize and live its unity on earth. "O Mother of Union," teach us always the paths that lead to union!

Enable us, in the future, to go to "meet all persons and all peoples," who on the paths" of diverse religions" seek God and want to serve Him. Help us all to announce Christ and to reveal "the Divine power and wisdom" hidden in His Cross. For you first revealed Him at Bethlehem not only to simple and faithful shepherds but also to the wise men of far-off countries!

SEASON OF CHRISTMAS

THERE WAS NO ROOM FOR THEM

ON Christmas eve, the Mother who was to bear a Son did not find a roof for herself.

She did not find the conditions that normally surround the great Divine yet human mystery of bringing a child to the light of day.

Allow me to use the logic of the faith and the logic of a consequent humanism. The event that I am speaking about is an immense cry, it is a permanent challenge to each and to all, especially perhaps in our age in which an expectant mother is asked to give a great proof of moral coherence.

Indeed, what is euphemistically termed "an interruption of pregnancy" (abortion) cannot be judged according to other authentically human categories than those of the moral law, that is, of conscience.

I could say much more about this subject—if not from the confidences expressed in confessionals, certainly from the confidences received by consultors for responsible motherhood.

"A VIRGIN ABOUT TO GIVE BIRTH"

WE cannot abandon a mother who is about to give birth; we cannot leave her to her doubts, difficulties, and temptations. We must stay by her side, so that she will have enough courage and faith, so that she will not harm her conscience, so that the most basic bond of respect for human beings will not be shattered.

This is the bond that exists from the moment of conception and that requires of us that we in a certain manner be with every mother who is to give birth; and we must offer these mothers every possible help.

Let us turn our eyes to Mary: the Virgin who is to give birth. Let us look to her, we who are the Church, and seek to understand better the responsibility that the Lord's birth bears in itself toward each person who is to be born on earth.

"SHE WAS WITH CHILD"

THE birth of Jesus Christ during the course of the night at Bethlehem is narrated by the Evangelist Luke.

The description is rather detailed. It responds first of all to the request for the "historical circumstances" in which the event had taken place. Hence, we learn that as a consequence of the decree of Caesar Augustus a census was ordered "while Quirinius was governor of Syria" (cf. Lk 2:1-2). With this as a backdrop the description of the event itself ensues.

Thus, to fulfill the duty deriving from the decision of the authority, Joseph "went from the town of Nazareth in Galilee to Judea, to the town of David, which is called Bethlehem . . . to register with Mary, his espoused wife." Joseph did this "because he was of the house and lineage of David."

The house and the lineage, as is known, were associated with the city of Bethlehem.

Evidently, the census had to be carried out at the place of origin of one's family.

Mary was expecting at the time. "She was with child."

SHE WRAPPED HER CHILD IN SWADDLING CLOTHES

ALL this is recounted in a detailed way in the description of the Evangelist Luke. "The description of the birth itself of the child" is also presented in detail and at the same time permeated with a total simplicity.

We learn that the event took place after their arrival in Bethlehem, "while they were there." We also know that it took place in unaccustomed conditions, "because there was no room for them in the inn" (Lk 2:7).

Hence, the coming of Mary's Son into the world took place "not in a house," which is the usual dwelling of human beings, but in "a dwelling" destined "for animals," since it is stated that Mary wrapped her Son in swaddling clothes "and laid Him in a manger" (Lk 2:7).

SHE LAID HIM IN A MANGER

BEHOLD, the time has come for a marvelous event: "The days for her to be delivered were fulfilled. She gave birth to her firstborn Son and wrapped Him in swaddling clothes and laid Him in a manger" (Lk 2:6-7).

We ask ourselves: Is this a common or an uncommon event? How many children are born on earth in the course of twenty-four hours, while in certain parts of the world it is day and in others night!

Certainly, every one of these moments is something out of the ordinary. It is something unique for a father and especially for a mother when a baby is born, particularly if it is a first baby, a firstborn!

THE FEAST OF THE MOTHER

THE event that takes place in a stable, in the rocky cave, has a dimension of profound intimacy: it is something that takes place "between" the Mother and the Child being born. No outsider has access to it. Even Joseph the carpenter of Nazareth remains a silent witness.

Mary alone is fully aware of her Motherhood. She alone understands what the cry of the Infant means to the just.

The birth of Christ is above all her mystery, her great day. It is a feast of the Mother.

THE WORD HAS BECOME FLESH

THE birth in the stable is a strange feast: without any sign of the liturgy of the synagogue, without readings from the Prophets, and without the chanting of any Psalms. "Sacrifice and oblation You did not desire, but a body You have prepared for Me" (Heb 10:5), He seems to say with His cry; although He was the Eternal Son, consubstantial with the Father, "God from God, Light from Light," He has become flesh (cf. Jn 1:14).

In that body He reveals Himself as one of us, a small Infant, in all its fragility and vulnerability. It is dependent on the solicitude of human beings, entrusted to their love, without defense. He cries, and the world does not hear Him; it cannot hear Him. The cry of a newborn child can barely be heard only a few steps away.

A CHILD IS BORN

THE Baby is born.
The Son is born.
He is born from His Mother.

For nine months, like every newborn child, He was tied to her womb. He is born "from His Mother" in time and in accord with the laws of human time for births. He is "born eternally from the Father." He is the Son of God. He is the Word.

He brings with Him into the world all the love of the Father for human beings. He is the revelation of the Divine Philanthropy. In Him the Father gives Himself to every person, and in Him is confirmed the eternal inheritance of human beings in God. In Him is revealed, to the very end, "the future of the human race." He speaks of the significance and the sense of human life, independently of any suffering or handicap that could weigh upon this life, in its earthly dimensions.

MARY'S "YES"

I WISH to offer for your reflection a consideration suggested to me by the difficult situation—terribly anguishing for a mother—in which Mary must have found herself in not being able to provide a roof over the Child to be born. The great and mysterious event of motherhood in so many women can lead to motives of suffering, doubt, and temptation.

The generous "Yes" that a woman must voice in the presence of the life that has germinated in her womb—a "Yes" often accompanied by the fear of a thousand difficulties—always entails an inner act of confidence in God and of trust in the new person who is to be born. With a fraternal sense of charity and solidarity, we must never leave to herself—especially if she is vacillating and filled with doubt—a woman who is preparing to bring forth a new person who shall be a brother or sister to each of us.

We must seek to give her every necessary help in her situation. We must strengthen to her and offer her courage and hope.

THE IMAGE OF THE MOTHER

A birth speaks always of the Mother, of the one who gives life, the one who brings the human being into the world.

We see her therefore—as in so many pictures and sculptures—with the Child in her arms, or with the Child on her lap. Mother, the one who has generated and nourished the Son of God. Mother of Christ. There is no image that is more known and that speaks in more telling fashion of the mystery of the birth of the Lord as the image of the Mother with Jesus in her arms.

Is it not precisely this image that forms the basis for our singular trust in Mary? Is it not precisely this image that enables us to live within the circle of all the mysteries of our faith and, on contemplating them as "Divine," to consider them so "human" at the same time?

But there is still another image of the Mother with the Son in her arms: "the Pieta." Mary with Jesus taken down from the Cross; with Jesus Who has expired before her eyes, on Mount Calvary, and after-death now returns to her arms on which at Bethlehem He was offered as Savior of the world.

WITH US SHE PRAYS FOR PEACE

I WOULD like to unite our prayer to that Motherhood that the Church venerates in a particular way on the Octave Day of the Lord's Nativity.

Tht is why I say: "O Mother, you know what it means to hold in your arms the lifeless body of your Son, the One to Whom you gave life. Spare all mothers on earth from the death of their children, from torments, slavery, the destruction of war, persecutions, concentration camps, and prisons!

"Preserve in them the joy of the birth, sustenance, development, and life of a human being. In the name of this life, in the name of the Birth of the Lord, pray with us for peace and justice in the world!"

THE MOTHER'S "PLACE"

DURING the Octave of Christmas, the Church turns the gaze of our mind toward the mystery of Motherhood. In this way, she highlights "the place" of the Mother, the maternal dimension, in the whole mystery of the birth of God.

This Mother bears the name of Mary. The Church venerates her in a particular way. The cult she renders to Mary surpasses the cult of all other saints (and is termed hyperdulia). The Church venerates Mary in this manner because she was the Mother; because she was chosen to be the Mother of God's Son; because she gave "a body" in time to that Son Who is the Eternal Word—at a moment in history she gave Him "humanity."

The Church inserts this particular veneration of the Mother of God throughout the whole cycle of the Liturgical Year, and in a discreet but also very solemn way she accentuates the moment of the human conception of the Son of God on the feast of the Annunciation on March 25, nine months before Christmas.

MARY WALKS WITH THE CHURCH

WE can say that during this period, from March 25 to December 25, the Church walks with Mary, who like every mother awaits the moment of birth: the day of Christmas. And at the same time, during this same period, Mary "walks" with the Church. Her motherly expectation is inscribed in a discreet manner in the life of the Church of each year.

Everything that takes place between Nazareth, Ain Karim, and Bethlehem becomes a theme for the Liturgy of Christ's life, for prayer, especially that of the Rosary, and for contemplation. No longer part of the Liturgical Year is a particular feast dedicated to "the Virgin about to Bear," the feast of the Expected Motherhood [Expectation] of the Virgin, which used to be celebrated on December 18.

"THE HOLY SPIRIT WILL COME UPON YOU"

IN inserting into the rhythm of her Liturgy the Mystery "of the Maternal Expectation of the Virgin," the Church meditates—under the inspiration of the mystery of these months that unite the moment of birth with the moment of conception—on the whole spiritual dimension of the Maternity of the Mother of God.

This "spiritual" Maternity ("quoad spiritus") began at the same time as the physical Maternity ("quoad corpus"). At the moment of the Annunciation Mary had this colloquy with the Announcer: "How shall this happen since I do not know man?" (Lk 1:34). He replied: "The Holy Spirit will come upon you and the power of the Most High will overshadow you; hence, the Holy Offspring to be born will be called the Son of God'" (Lk 1:35).

MOTHER OF HUMAN BEINGS

CONTEMPORANEOUSLY with the physical Maternity of Mary ("quoad corpus"), her spiritual Maternity ("quoad spiritus") began.

Thus, this Maternity filled the nine months of expectation for the moment of birth, as well as the thirty years spent in Bethlehem, Egypt, and Nazareth. It also filled the later years during which Jesus, after leaving His house at Nazareth, taught the Gospel of the Kingdom, years that came to a close with the events of Calvary and with the Cross.

There, the "spiritual" Maternity in a certain sense reached its key moment. "Seeing His Mother there with the disciple whom He loved, Jesus said to His Mother, 'Woman, there is your son' " (Jn 19:26). Thus, in a new way, He has united her, His own Mother, with human beings; with those to whom He had transmitted the Gospel. He united her with every person. He united her with the

Church, on the day of the latter's birth in history, the day of Pentecost.

From that day, the whole Church has her as Mother. And all human beings have her as Mother. They understand the words pronounced from the height of the Cross as addressed to each of them. Mother of all human beings. The spiritual Maternity knows no limits. It extends in time and space. It reaches so many human hearts. It reaches all nations.

AN ETERNAL VOCATION

DURING the Season of Christmas the Church brings Mary's Motherhoood before the eyes of our mind, and she does so on the first day of the new year. She does this also to highlight the dignity of every mother, to define and recall the meaning of motherhood, not only in the life of every person but also in all human cultures.

Motherhood is a woman's vocation, and it is also a contemporaneous vocation. "The Mother who understands everything and, with her heart, embraces each of us": these are the words of a song sung by young people in Poland that came to my mind at this moment. The song goes on to announce that today the world in a special way "hungers and thirsts" for that motherhood which "physically" and "spiritually" is a woman's vocation, as it is the vocation of Mary.

SO THAT A WOMAN WILL DESERVE LOVE

WE must do everything possible so that the dignity of this splendid maternal vocation will not suffer in the inner life of new generations; so that the authority of the woman-mother will not be diminished in family, social, and public life as well as in our whole civilization: in all contemporary legislation, in the organization of work, in publications, in the culture of daily life, and in education and study. In every sphere of life. This is a basic criterion.

We must do everything possible so that a woman will deserve love and generation. We must do everything possible so that children, family, and society will see in a woman the dignity that Christ saw in her.

Mother of God, our hope!

"JESUS" SIGNIFIES "GOD SAVES"

LET us rejoice in "the Divine Motherhood of Mary." Let us address her, as always, with the words of the Angelic Salutation: "Blessed are you among women and blessed is the fruit of your womb, Jesus" (cf. Lk 1:42).

Today is the octave day of the solemnity of Christmas. Precisely on this day, "the Child was called Jesus, the Name the Angel had given Him before He was conceived" (Lk 2:21).

The Name Jesus signifies "God saves" (Jehoshua). It means "Savior." Precisely in this Name is the world saved. In this Name humankind is saved.

THE FULLNESS OF TIME

CHRISTMAS is the greatest feast of Mary. It is at this very moment that she presents herself as the Mother of God. The fullness of time also signifies her Divine Motherhood.

At the same time, this Motherhood—like all human motherhood—is synonymous with a beginning. Motherhood signifies the beginning of life, the beginning of a human being.

Mary's Motherhood signifies the beginning of the God-Man in the history of humankind. And this is precisely "the fullness of time."

THE VIRGINAL MOTHERHOOD OF MARY

"THE Motherhood" of Mary is "virginal." Through the working of the Holy Spirit she has conceived and given to the world the Son of God, without "knowing man." St. Paul explains this mystery of Mary's Motherhood by making references to "the eternal Fatherhood of God":

"When the fullness of time had come, God sent forth His Son born of a woman" (Gal 4:4).

The virginal Motherhood of the Mother of God corresponds to the eternal Fatherhood of God. It is found, in a certain sense, along the way of the "mission of the Son," Who comes from the Father to humankind through His Mother.

Mary's Motherhood opens the way—"it opens the way of God to humankind."

It is, in a certain sense, the culmination of the way.

BROTHERS AND SISTERS ALL

WE know that the way of this maternal mission—once opened in human history—remains forever. It actualizes, through the history of humankind, the salvific mission of the Son of God: "the mission" that is consummated with the Cross and the Resurrection. And together with the mission of the Son there remains in the history of humankind "the salvific Motherhood" of the earthly Mother: Mary of Nazareth.

The Fatherhood of God says to all of us "that we are brothers and sisters."

For all humankind, Mary's Motherhood adds a particular familial aspect.

We have the right to think of, speak of, and regard ourselves as "the human family." We are all brothers and sisters in this family.

HE SENT FORTH HIS SON BORN OF A WOMAN

DOES not the Apostle Paul clearly say all this in today's Liturgy?

"God sent forth His Son born of a woman . . . so that we might become His adopted children" (Gal 4:4-5).

"God has sent forth into our hearts the Spirit of His Son Who calls out: 'Abba, Father' " (Gal 4:6).

"You are no longer a slave but a son! And if you are a son you are also an heir, by God's design" (Gal 4:7).

This adoptive filiation is the great inheritance left us by the birth of God. "It is the reality of the Grace of the Redemption." At the same time, it is a basic and central point of reference for all humankind, for all persons, if it is true that we must speak "of the universal brotherhood and sisterhood of all human beings and peoples."

INCARNATE IN THE VIRGIN'S WOMB

IN the contemplation of the mystery of the Incarnation, the Son of God cannot be separated from His Mother. That is why in the formulation of her faith the Church proclaims that the Son "by the power of the Holy Spirit . . . was born of the Virgin Mary, and became Man."

When at the Council of Ephesus the title "Theotokos," Mother of God, was applied to Mary, it was the intention of the Council Fathers to guarantee "the truth of the mystery of the Incarnation."

They wished to affirm the personal unity of Christ, God and Man, a unity of such a kind that Mary's Motherhood with regard to Jesus was by this very fact a Motherhood with regard to the Son of God. Mary is the "Mother of God" because her Son is God; she is Mother only in the order of human generation, but since the Child conceived by her and placed in the world is God, she must be called "Mother of God!"

THE WORD HAS BECOME MAN

THE affirmation of the Divine Motherhood enlightens us concerning the "meaning of the Incarnation." It shows how the Word, a Divine Person, has become man: He has done so through the cooperation of a woman in the working of the Holy Spirit.

A woman has been associated, in a singular manner, in the mystery of the Savior's coming into the world.

Through the intermediary of this woman, Jesus intimately united Himself to the human generations that preceded His birth. Thanks to Mary, He has a "real birth" and His life on earth begins exactly like that of every other human being.

By her Motherhood, Mary enables the Son of God to have—after the extraordinary conception through the working of the Holy Spirit—a human development and a normal insertion into the society of human beings.

THE DIGNITY OF MARY

THE title "Mother of God," while it highlights the humanity of Jesus in the Incarnation, also draws attention "to the supreme dignity accorded to a creature."

It is understandable that in the history of doctrine there was a moment in which such dignity encountered some opposition: it could in effect seem difficult to admit this because of the dizzying heights it opened up.

But when the title of "Theotokos" was put to discussion, the Church reacted promptly, confirming its attribution to Mary as a truth of faith. Those who believe that Jesus is "God" cannot fail to believe that Mary is "Mother of God."

The dignity conferred on Mary shows "how far God has willed to push reconciliation."

ALLIED WITH GOD

IMMEDIATELY after the first sin, God had announced His intention of concluding an alliance with the woman so as to assure victory over the enemy of the human race: "I will put enmity between you and the woman, and between your offspring and hers; He will crush your head, while you strike at His heel" (Gn 3:15).

According to this oracle, the woman was destined to become God's ally in the struggle against the devil. She was to be the mother of the One Who was to crush the head of the enemy.

Nevertheless, in the prophetic perspective of the Old Testament, this Offspring of the woman Who was to triumph over the spirit of evil seemed to be no more than a man.

Here the marvelous reality of the Incarnation intervenes. The woman's Descendant Who fulfills the prophetic oracle is not simply a man.

He is indeed fully a man thanks to the woman whose Son He is, but He is also true God at the same time.

The strict alliance at the beginning between God and the woman assures a new dimension. Mary enters into this alliance as Mother of God's Son.

AN ADMIRABLE EDUCATRIX

WE are forever astounded that a woman could have been called to bring into the world the One Who is God, that she could have received the mission to rear Him as every mother rears her child, that she could have prepared the Savior with a motherly education for His future work. "Mary was a mother in the full sense," and because of this she was also "an admirable educatrix."

The fact, confirmed by the Gospel, that during His infancy Jesus was subject to her (Lk 2:51) indicates that her motherly presence had a profound influence on the human development of the Son of God.

This is one of the most striking aspects of the mystery of the Incarnation.

MARY ENABLES US TO GRASP THE GREATNESS OF GOD'S LOVE

IN the dignity conferred in a most singular fashion on Mary, there is manifested the dignity that the mystery of the Word made flesh intends to confer on all humankind.

When the Son of God humbled Himself to become a man, like us in all things except sin, He raised humankind to the level of God.

In the reconciliation worked between God and humankind, He did not desire simply to reestablish the integrity and purity of human life, which had been wounded by sin.

He wanted to communicate the Divine Life to human beings and grant them full access to familiarity with God.

In this way, Mary enables us to grasp the greatness of God's love, not only for her but also for us.

She introduces us to the grand work of God, Who did not limit Himself to healing the human race of the plague of sin but assigned to it a superior destiny of intimate union with Himself.

A NEW FAMILY

THE birth of the Baby during the night of Bethlehem has formed a new family. That is why the Sunday within the octave of Christmas is the feast of the Family of Nazareth.

It is the Holy Family, because it has been fashioned for the birth of Jesus, Whom even His "Adversary" will be constrained to proclaim "the Holy One of God" (Mk 1:24).

It is the Holy Family, because the holiness of the One Who was born has become the source of a singular sanctification for both His Virgin-Mother and St. Joseph her husband. As the lawful husband, he was regarded by people as the father of the Baby born during the census at Bethlehem.

THE HOLY FAMILY

THIS Family is thus a human Family. Hence, during the time of Christmas the Church addresses all human beings through the Holy Family.

Holiness imprints on this Family, in which the Son of God came to the world, a unique, exceptional, unrepeatable, and supernatural character.

At the same time, everything that we can say about every human family—about its duties, and its difficulties—we can say about this Holy Family too.

Indeed, this Holy Family is truly poor. At the moment of Jesus' birth it does not even have a roof over its head. It will soon be forced into exile; then after the danger has passed, it will remain a family that lives modestly, in poverty, by the labor of its hands.

THE MEETING PLACE

THE condition of the family of Mary is similar to that of many human families. It is the meeting place for our own solidarity with every family, with every community of a man and a woman in which another human being is born.

It is a Family that does not remain only on our altars as an object of praise and veneration. Through so many episodes known to us from the Gospels of St. Luke and St. Matthew it comes near, in a certain sense, to every human family. It also experiences those profound problems—delightful but at the same time difficult—that conjugal and family life carries with it.

When we read attentively what the Evangelists (especially Matthew) have written about the events that Joseph and Mary lived through before the birth of Jesus, the problems to which we have alluded become even more evident.

THE DIGNITY OF PARENTS

THE solemnity of Christmas and, in its context, the feast of the Holy Family are especially near and dear, precisely because in them we encounter the fundamental dimension of our faith, that is, the mystery of the Incarnation, and the equally fundamental dimension of human development. Everyone must realize that this essential dimension of human development is precisely the family.

And in the family the essential dimension is procreation: a new human being is conceived and born, and through this conception and this birth the man and woman in their capacity as husband and wife become mother and father, parents, acquiring a new dignity and assuming new duties.

THE FAMILY IS IRREPLACEABLE

FROM many points of view, these fundamental duties are of the greatest importance.

Not only from the point of view of the concrete community that is their family but also from the point of view of every human community, every society, Nation, State, school, profession, and circle. Everything depends in principle on the way parents and family have fulfilled their first and fundamental duties, on the way and in the measure that they have taught "to be human" that creature who thanks to them has become a human being, has obtained "humanity."

In this the family is irreplaceable. Everything must be done to insure that the family will not be replaced. This is demanded not only by the "private" good of every person but also by the common good of every society, Nation, and State on any continent.

THE FAMILY OF JESUS

THE Family of Jesus, Mary, and Joseph is a holy Family above all because of the holiness of the One for Whom it was formed as a human family; indeed in it we see elements proper to so many other human families.

As the Gospel indicates, this Family is truly poor—at the moment of the birth of the Son of God, during the period of exile in Egypt that it was forced to endure, and at Nazareth where it lived modestly from manual labor.

Jesus, Mary, and Joseph provide a wonderful example of human solidarity, communion with all other families, and insertion into the fuller human context that is society.

Every other human family must pattern itself on this Divine Model and live after its example to resolve the difficult problems of conjugal and familial life. Such profound and vital problems must be confronted with solidary and responsible action.

AS AT NAZARETH

A S at Nazareth, so in every family, God is rendered present and is inserted into human developments.

For the family, which is the union of man and woman, is by its nature directed toward the procreation of new human beings. These new beings are then accompanied into existence by a diligent educational effort that assures their physical but above all spiritual and moral growth.

The family is thus the privileged place and the sanctuary in which the whole grand and intimate development of each unrepeatable human person takes place.

Hence, the family is entrusted with fundamental duties, whose generous fulfillment cannot fail to enrich greatly the persons responsible for the family itself. They become God's most closest collaborators in the formation of new human beings.

HIDDEN IN CHRIST

I N the house of Nazareth, Jesus was subject (Lk 2:51); He was subject to both Joseph and Mary as "every child is subject to its parents."

The years go by in the hidden life of the Holy Family at Nazareth.

The Son of God—sent by the Father—is hidden from the world, hidden from all human beings, even those closest to Jesus. Only Mary and Joseph know

His Mystery. They live in its circle. They live the Mystery daily. In the eyes of others, the Son of the eternal Father passes for their Son, "the carpenter's Son" (Mt 13:55)

The Son of God, the Incarnate Word, remained hidden for thirty years of His earthly life.

At the same time, Mary and Joseph remained "hidden in Christ," in His Mystery and in His mission.

THEY FOUND THE CHILD WITH MARY

HOW great is the faith of the Magi! How certain they are about the light that the Spirit of the Lord has shone in their hearts! How tenaciously they follow Him! With what coherence they seek the newborn Messiah!

And when at last they reached their goal, "they were overjoyed. . . . And entering the house, they found the Child with Mary His Mother. They prostrated themselves and worshiped Him. Then they opened their treasures and offered Him gifts of gold, frankincense, and myrrh" (Mt 2:10-11).

The light of faith has enabled them to scrutinize all unknown things. Unknown roads and unknown circumstances.

For example, when they found themselves in the presence of the Newborn—a human newborn Child with no roof over His head—they noted the miserable state of the place.

What a contrast with their position as men of learning and great social influence.

Yet "they prostrated themselves and worshiped Him" (cf. Mt 2:11).

MARY BEGINS HER WORK OF EVANGELIZATION

WHILE celebrating the luminous manifestation of the Savior to the Gentiles and the universal vocation to Salvation, the Church also contemplates the Virgin Mother who offers her Son for the adoration of the Magi.

Indeed, from antiquity the Epiphany has been regarded as a significant moment of the Savior's Incarnation and hence also of Mary's Divine Motherhood.

But in the event recounted for us by St. Matthew (Mt 2:11) at the moment when Mary presents her Son to the Magi, she not only performs a personal action as Mother but also acts as the figure of the Church. As the mother of all peoples, the Church in the person of Mary initiates her work of evangelization.

PROTOTYPE OF THE CHURCH

THIS personal and ecclesial signification of the virginal Motherhood of Mary inspires us once again to fix our attention on the Virgin-Mother in order to deepen the ecclesial value of this mystery.

Mary is the prototype of the Church in her Virginal Motherhood, an essential mystery that unites her to the Church in a common vocation and mission.

Christ, as the Second Vatican Council declares, is born of the Virgin Mary by the working of the Holy Spirit, so that He may in a certain sense continue to be born and grow in the Church, always by the working of the Holy Spirit.

Both Mary and the Church are living temples, sanctuaries, and instruments by whom and in whom the Holy Spirit is manifested.

They engender in a virginal manner the same Savior: Mary bears life in her womb and engenders it virginally; the Church confers life in the baptismal water and in the announcement of the faith, engendering it in the hearts of the faithful.

MOTHER AND VIRGIN

IN the mystery of the Church, which in its turn is justly called Mother and Virgin, the Blessed Virgin Mary is the first to give the example of virgin and mother, and she does so in an eminent way.

In this strict typological relationship, the Motherhood of Mary receives light and significance from the motherhood of the Church, of which she is a member and a figure. By the same token, the motherhood of the Church receives light and takes its real beginning from the Motherhood of Mary, in which she feels already perfectly realized.

Like Mary, the Church is also a virgin, and in engendering children of God she integrally maintains faith, hope, and charity.

The virginal motherhood that Mary and the Church have in common makes of them an indispensable and indissoluble unity, as in a single sacrament of salvation for all human beings.

FAITH IS NEVER EASY

DURING the Season of Advent and in the feasts of Christmas, we have lengthily contemplated, alongside Christ, the Virgin Mary.

We have drawn near to the mystery of Christmas and have found the Child with Mary, "the Child and His Mother" (Mt 2:11, 13).

Adoring the Son, we have venerated the Mother, proclaiming her blessed before all and above all because of her faith (cf. Lk 1:45; 11:28).

Faith is never easy, and it was certainly not easy for Mary.

This is emphasized by the numerous praises heaped on her because of her faith: they highlight the value, the cost, and especially the difficulty of her faith.

On the other hand, the words of the Evangelist underline this point in a more explicit fashion: "But they did not understand what He said to them" (Lk 2:50).

THE "INCOMPREHENSION" OF MARY

L UKE is not afraid to point up the difficulty Mary and Joseph have with the words and the mystery of their Son, as well as their incomprehension.

The "incomprehension" of Mary, Joseph, and the disciples in general is far different from the unbelief of those without faith in Jesus.

It is a question of difficulty in penetrating deeply, and quickly, into the unfathomable depth of the person and mystery of Christ.

But it is a momentary "incomprehension," which leads to reflection, meditation, and an attitude of wisdom so characteristic of the Mother of Jesus, who conserved and meditated on the words and events in her heart (cf. Lk 2:19, 51).

SEASON OF LENT

FAITH IS A LIGHT

FAITH is indeed a light, but it is not an all-encompassing understanding of the mystery. On the contrary, it is a trust in God and in His word that transcends the limits of human reason. This stems from the fact that faith relies on God, seeking and finding in such an attitude its strength and its confidence.

This is Mary's inner disposition, expressed once and for all in the Annunciation: "I am the servant of the Lord. Let it be done to me as you say." Mary's faith is great, a faith that has been tested and is blessed: it is the faith of those who have not seen and yet have believed (cf. Jn 20:29).

The Virgin's earthly existence, like our own, proceeds day by day, in faith and not in sight. "Thus, even the Blessed Virgin," says the Council, "made progress in the pilgrimage of faith and faithfully preserved her union with her Son even to the Cross" (LG 58).

May she who believed accompany us along the mysterious pathways of God!

DO WHATEVER JESUS TELLS YOU

WE beg you,
look upon the wretchedness of your children
as you did at Cana
when you took to heart the situation of that family.
Today the greatest poverty of the family that is
　yours

is the lack of priestly, diaconal, religious, and missionary vocations.

May your "all-powerful supplication" touch the heart

of many of our brothers and sisters

so that they may listen to, grasp, and respond to the Lord's call.

Repeat to them in the depths of their hearts

what you said to the waiters of Cana:

Do whatever Jesus tells you (cf. Jn 2:5).

THE PRESENTATION OF THE LORD

"THE Presentation of the Lord." If we want to fully appreciate all the rich content of this feast, we must "consider it as a joint commemoration of the Son and of the Mother. It is the celebration of the mystery of salvation accomplished by Christ, a mystery with which the Blessed Virgin was intently associated as the Mother of the Suffering Servant of Yahweh, as the one who performs a mission belonging to ancient Israel, and as the model of the new People of God, which is ever being tested in its faith and hope by suffering and persecution" *(Marialis Cultus: Devotion to the Blessed Virgin Mary, 7).*

CARRIED IN MARY'S ARMS

"AND suddenly there will come to the Temple the Lord Whom you seek. . . . Yes, He is coming" (Mal 3:1).

Carried in the arms of Mary and Joseph, He comes as a forty-day-old Infant for the purpose of fulfilling the prescriptions of the Mosaic Law.

They bring Him into the Temple like so many other Israelite infants: the child of poor parents. Hence, He enters unobserved and—as if in contrast to the words of the Prophet Malachi—not expected by anyone.

"Deus absconditus"—a hidden God (cf. Is 45: 15). Hidden by human flesh, born in a state on the outskirts of the town of Bethlehem.

Subjected to the law of redemption as His Mother is subjected to the law of purification.

"A SWORD SHALL PIERCE YOUR OWN SOUL"

SIMEON speaks to Mary, first about her Son: "This Child is destined for the fall and the rise of many in Israel, to be a sign of contradiction."

Then he adds words about her: "And a sword shall pierce your own soul so that the thoughts of many hearts may be laid bare" (Lk 2:34-35).

This day is the feast of Jesus Christ, on the fortieth day of His life, in the Temple of Jerusalem where He was brought to satisfy the prescriptions of the Mosaic Law (cf. Lk 2:22-24). And it is also the feast of Mary.

She carries the Infant in her arms. But even in her arms Jesus is the light of our souls, the light that illumines the darkness of human knowledge and existence, of mind and heart.

The thoughts of many hearts are revealed when Mary's motherly arms carry this great Divine Light, when they bring Jesus close to human beings.

POOR BANISHED CHILDREN OF EVE

O beautiful Lady!
O Woman clothed with the sun!
Help us to penetrate your mystery:
—the mystery of the Virgin Mother,
—the mystery of the Servant Queen,
—the mystery of the Almighty Who asks.

Help us to discover ever more profoundly in this mystery the Christ, Redeemer of the world, Redeemer of human beings.

You are clothed with the sun, with the sun of the inscrutable Divinity, with the sun of the impenetrable Trinity.

"Full of grace" . . .

And at the same time, for us who are living on this earth, poor banished children of Eve, you are clothed with the sun of the Christ of Bethlehem and Nazareth, of Jerusalem and Calvary. You are clothed with the sun of the Redemption of the human race and the world through Your Son's Cross and Resurrection.

Grant that this sun may always shine for us on this earth!

Grant that this sun may never be obscured in people's hearts!

"BLESSED ARE YOU AMONG WOMEN"

"**B**LESSED are you among women, and blessed is the fruit of your womb!" (Lk 1:42).

The words that Elizabeth addressed to the Blessed Virgin on the day of the visitation rise spontaneously to our lips as we indicate our gratitude to the heavenly Mother for all that she has done and continues to do in that "spiritual crossroads" of the modern world that is the city of Lourdes.

MARY IS PRESENT IN OUR MIDST

MARY is spiritually present in our midst. We look to her with the same eyes with which Elizabeth looked to her when she saw Mary arrive in haste and heard her greeting: "The moment your greeting sounded in my ears, the baby leapt for joy in my womb" (Lk 1:44).

How can we fail to accept this first invitation to reflect? Elizabeth's transport of joy underlines the gift that can be contained "in a simple greeting," when the greeting comes from a heart filled with God.

Very often the abyss of solitude that oppresses a soul can be dissipated by the luminous ray of a smile and a kind word!

MARY FILLS ELIZABETH'S HEART WITH JOY

A GOOD word is quickly voiced; yet we find it difficult to pronounce at times. We are impeded by fatigue, we are distracted from doing so by our preoccupations, and we are held back by a feeling of coldness or egoistic indifference.

So it happens that we pass by persons we know and do not look them in the face; we do not take account of how much they are suffering from the subtle pain that afflicts those who feel ignored.

A cordial word or an affectionate gesture would suffice to awaken something in them: a nod of attention and courtesy can be a breath of fresh air in a closed existence, overwhelmed by sadness and discouragement.

Mary's greeting fills her cousin Elizabeth's heart with joy.

THE FAITH OF MARY

"BLESSED is she who has believed that the Lord's words to her would be fulfilled" (Lk

1:45). This is what Elizabeth said in reply to Our Lady's greeting. These words were dictated by the Holy Spirit (cf. Lk 1:41). They spotlight Mary's principal virtue: faith.

The Fathers of the Church meditated at length on the meaning of this virtue in the spiritual development of the Blessed Virgin, and they did not hesitate to express evaluations about it that may seem surprising to us.

It is enough to cite Augustine for all: "Mary's quality as a mother would have been of no value to her if she had not borne Christ more intensely in her heart than in her body!"

MARY HAS BELIEVED IN THE IMPOSSIBLE PROJECT

THANKS to her faith, Mary could look without fear into the uncharted abyss of God's salvific plan. It was not easy to believe that God could "become flesh" and come "to dwell among us" (cf. Jn 1:14); that He wished to hide Himself in our insignificant daily life, clothing Himself in our human fragility and subject to so many and so humiliating conditions.

Mary dared to believe in this "impossible" project. She trusted in the Almighty and became the principal collaborator of that wondrous Divine initiative that reopened our history to hope.

Christians are also called to a similar attitude of faith, which leads them to look courageously "beyond" the possibilities and limitations of a purely human event.

They know they can rely on God to affirm His own sovereign freedom in the confrontations with human conditions; and very often He chooses the weak things of the world and the despised in order to confound the wise and the strong, "so that no one can do any boasting before God" (1 Cor 1:29).

THE DESIGNS OF PROVIDENCE

IN the two thousand years of history that have passed since that time we can discover striking confirmation of the singular action of God, which even today leaves perplexed all those who seek purely human explanations for the designs of Providence. It suffices to mention St. Bernadette in this respect.

However, incomparably more numerous are the human tribulations whose social importance remains hidden from us. There are those countless souls who have spent their lives in giving of themselves in the anonymity of home, factory, and office; who have consumed themselves in prayer in the solitude of the cloister; who have immolated themselves in the daily martyrdom of sickness.

The time will come when Christ's Second Coming will be unveiled, and it will become apparent in all clarity what role these souls played in the development of the history of the world. This will also be a reason for joy, who will make it a subject of eternal praise of the thrice holy God.

THE "MAGNIFICAT"

HERE below, a foretaste of that joy is granted to the "little ones" to whom the Lord reveals His plans (cf. Mt 11:25). Mary guides the phalanx of "little ones" who have the wisdom of God in their hearts. That is why she was able to proclaim in the presence of Elizabeth the canticle of the "Magnificat," which over the centuries will be the purest expression of the joy that streams forth from every faithful soul.

"Mary's canticle must become the canticle of every day of our lives": indeed, there is no human situation that cannot find therein an adequate interpretation.

The Blessed Virgin gave voice to this canticle even though her spirit was assailed by questions. These questions concerned the reaction of her husband to her situation, since he was still unaware of God's part in it. They also concerned the future of her Son, about Whom disquieting prophetic words had been spoken (cf. Is 53).

THE SENTIMENTS OF MARY

WE can sing the Magnificat with inner exultation of spirit if we seek to have in us "the sentiments of Mary": her faith, her humility, her candor.

It is precisely this that Ambrose, the saintly bishop of Milan, exhorts us to do: "May the soul of Mary be in all of us to magnify the Lord; may the spirit of Mary be in all of us to find joy in God."

If we learn to heed her voice, she will give us the words to do this: "As a mother comforts her child, so will I comfort you. In Jerusalem you shall find your comfort" (Is 66:13).

THE LORD'S POWER SHALL BE MADE KNOWN

WE know which Jerusalem is in question here. It is the Jerusalem "on high" (Gal 4: 26), which John saw "coming down out of heaven from God, made ready as a bride adorned for her husband" (Rv 21:2).

It is toward this Jerusalem that we raise our eyes and on her that we set our hopes, because it is in her that there will finally be fulfilled the prophetic promise that we have heard: "Your bodies shall flourish like the grass; the Lord's power shall be made known to His servants" (Is 66:14)

"THE MESSAGE OF MERCY"

"BLESSED are you among women" (Lk 1:42). This evocative Marian greeting, which repeats and echoes down the centuries the greeting that Elizabeth, "filled with the Holy Spirit," addressed "in a loud voice" to the Virgin Mother of

God, seems to be especially suited to honor and celebrate the Blessed Virgin Mary on the day that commemorates her appearance in the Grotto of Massabielle to entrust the humble Bernadette with a message of grace and mercy.

Who can say that such a message does not retain its full value for our day? Making use of that unknown child, Mary intended above all to recall sinners to conversion, soliciting for them and their salvation the communitary commitment of all the Christian faithful.

"BLESSED IS THE FRUIT OF YOUR WOMB"

"BLESSED are you among women": this greeting, which we address to Mary in order to honor her by repeating the "inspired" words of Elizabeth, would be incomplete unless it were followed by the other words that—as the Gospel indicates—were pronounced shortly afterward in the house of Zechariah.

Just as Elizabeth in no way separated mother and child but rather associated them intimately by adding the words "et benedictus fructus ventris tui" ("and blessed is the fruit of your womb"), so we too must address ourselves to the Lord Jesus with the promptitude of a lively faith and the strength of an ardent love.

For us, too, the content of the expression "ad Jesum per Mariam" ("To Jesus through Mary") must be revealed as true. It "must be fully realized," so that the liturgical commemoration itself will be the occasion and the means for us to draw nearer to Jesus and to confess that He is "the fruit of Mary's womb."

AT MARY'S INVITATION

WHY is it precisely the sick who make the pilgrimage to Lourdes?

Why, we ask ourselves, has that place become for them like a "Cana of Galilee," to which they feel invited in a particular way?

What draws them to Lourdes with such force?

The answer must be sought in the Word of God.

At Cana there was a wedding feast, a feast of joy because it was a feast of love.

We can easily imagine the "atmosphere" that reigned in the banquet hall.

Even that joy, however, like every other human reality, was "an insidious joy."

The spouses did not know it but their feast was about to be transformed into a small drama because the wine had run out.

And if we truly reflect on it, this was only the sign of all the other risks to which their beginning love was to undergo successive exposure.

Happily for them, "the Mother of Jesus was there" and so Jesus . . . had likewise been "invited to the marriage" (cf. Jn 2:1-2); and at the invitation of His Mother, Jesus immediately changed water into wine.

THE MOTHER OF JESUS IS THERE

THE banquet of Cana speaks to us of another banquet: the banquet of life, in which all of us desire to have a seat so as to taste a bit of joy.

The human heart is made for joy, and we must never be surprised that all of us need to attain this goal.

However, reality subjects so many persons to the crucifying experience of sorrow, sickness, mourning and tragedies, hereditary tares, solitude, physical tortures or moral anguish—an ensemble of "concrete cases," every one of which has a name, a face, and a story.

If these persons are animated by faith, they journey to Lourdes.

Why? Because they know that, as at Cana, "the Mother of Jesus is there": and where she is, her Son cannot be lacking.

MARY ENABLES US TO HEAR THE VOICE OF HER SON

THE salvific power of Christ propitiated by the intercession of His Mother is revealed at Lourdes "above all in the spiritual plane."

It is in the heart of the sick person that Mary enables the wonderworking voice of her Son to be heard: a voice that miraculously melts the hardening of bitterness and rebellion and restores eyes to the soul to see the world, others, and one's own destiny in a new light.

The sick "discover at Lourdes the inestimable value of their suffering." In the light of faith they succeed in seeing the fundamental meaning that suffering can have not only in their lives, interiorly renovated by such a flame that consumes and transforms, but also in the life of the Church, the Mystical Body of Christ.

SIGN OF SURE HOPE

ON Calvary, the Blessed Virgin Mary remained courageously standing at the foot of the Cross of her Son and participated personally in His Passion. She knows how to convince ever new souls to unite their own sufferings to the sacrifice of Christ in an "offertory" chorale that, transcending time and space, embraces all humankind and saves it.

Like the radiant morning star, she shines before the eyes of our faith "as a sign of sure hope and consolation until the Day of the Lord shall come" (LG 68). As pilgrims in this "valley of tears," we sigh to her: "And after this our exile show unto us the fruit of your womb, Jesus. O clement, O loving, O sweet Virgin Mary."

"THEY HAVE NO MORE WINE"

THE Gospel brings before our minds the event that took place at "Cana in Galilee": the wedding feast of Cana. During the banquet, the wine runs short. Then "Mary" turns to Christ with these words: "They have no more wine" (Jn 2:3).

By means of this ordinary fact, the Church wants to teach us that Mary is the Mother of Divine Providence, that is, "the one who watches over our human existence."

As Mother of all (cf. LG 61), as exemplar and type of the Church (LG 63), she watches over her children. And she encourages us to strive to build up the world in love, understanding, and justice, so that temporal reality may be more worthy of human beings (GS 93).

She continues to intercede for her children so that they will not neglect their temporal duties of fidelity to God and human beings (cf. GS 43), while she continues to obtain for them from the Redeemer "the gifts of eternal salvation" (LG 62).

MOTHER OF DIVINE PROVIDENCE

AT the wedding feast of Cana, Jesus replies to His Mother's words: "Woman, why do you involve Me? My hour has not yet come" (Jn 2:4).

Without hesitating, despite the negative-sounding response, the Mother of Jesus says to the servants: "Do whatever He tells you" (Jn 2:5).

And indeed Jesus orders the servants to fill with water six water jars nearby, and the water is transformed into wine. In the face of this miracle, the Evangelist notes: "Jesus worked this first of His signs at Cana in Galilee. Thus did He manifest His glory, and His disciples believed in Him" (Jn 2:11).

"The Mother of Divine Providence" also reveals herself in the words "Do whatever He tells you." This unveils Mary's essential function: to lead human beings to do the will of the Father manifested in Christ, to bring her children toward the center of the salvific mystery of the Redeemer of the human race.

"DO NOT BE AFRAID TO TAKE MARY AS YOUR WIFE"

"JOSEPH, son of David, do not be afraid to take Mary as your wife, because what is conceived in her is from the Holy Spirit. She is to have a Son, and you are to name Him Jesus because He will save His people from their sins" (Mt 1:20-21).

We find these words in the first chapter of the Gospel according to Matthew. Especially in the second part, they sound very similar to those that Miriam (that is, Mary) heard at the moment of the Incarnation.

Those words were pronounced at Nazareth "to a Virgin betrothed to a man named Joseph, of the house of David. The Virgin's name was Mary" (Lk 1:27).

The description of the Annunciation is found in the Gospel according to Luke.

Subsequently, Matthew mentions anew that after the marriage of Mary and Joseph, "before they came together, she was found to be with child through the power of the Holy Spirit" (Mt 1:18).

JOSEPH, AN UPRIGHT MAN

THIS way there was accomplished in Mary the mystery that had begun at the moment of the Annunciation, the moment in which the Virgin gave her response to the words of Gabriel: "Behold, I am the servant of the Lord. Let it be done to me as you say" (Lk 1:38).

When Joseph became aware of the mysterious maternity of Mary, as "an upright man" he was "unwilling to expose her to reproach" but "decided to send her away in secret" (Mt 1:19), Matthew's account goes on to say.

Right then Joseph, spouse of Mary and her husband in the eyes of the law, receives his personal "Annunciation."

During the night he hears the words that constitute an "explanation" and at the same time an invitation on the part of God: "Do not be afraid to take Mary as your wife" (Mt 1:20).

A VIRGIN ENGAGED TO JOSEPH

THE reading of the Gospel according to St. Matthew invites us to meditate on a particular moment in the life of Joseph of Nazareth, a moment filled with Divine content as well as deep human truth.

We read: "Now this is how the birth of Jesus Christ came about. When His Mother Mary was engaged to Joseph, but before they came together, she was found with child through the power of the Holy Spirit" (Mt 1:18).

When we hear these words they bring to mind those other well-known words that we recite daily in the Angelus prayer offered in the morning, at midday, and in the evening: "The Angel of the Lord declared unto Mary, and she conceived of the Holy Spirit."

THE MYSTERY OF MARY

THE Son of God was conceived by the power of the Holy Spirit in order to become man: the Son of Mary. This was the mystery of the Holy Spirit and of Mary. It was the mystery of the Virgin, who in response to the words of the Annunciation said: "Behold, I am the servant of the Lord. Let it be done to me as you say" (Lk 1:38).

That is what took place: "The Word was made flesh and dwelt among us" (Jn 1:14). And above all He came to dwell in the womb of the Virgin who—remaining a virgin—became a mother: "She was found to be with child through the power of the Holy Spirit" (Mt 1:18).

"This was the mystery of Mary."

A PROFOUND MYSTERY

"JOSEPH was unaware of this mystery." He did not know that in his spouse—although in accord with Jewish law he had not yet taken her into his home—was fulfilled the "promise of faith" made to Abraham, about which St. Paul speaks. He did not know that there was fulfilled in her, in Mary of the line of David, the prophecy that the Prophet Nathan once addressed to David.

This was the prophecy and the promise of faith whose fulfillment was awaited by the whole People, the Israel of the Divine election, and all humankind.

This was the mystery of Mary. Joseph was unaware of this mystery. Mary could not communicate it to him because it was a mystery beyond the capacity of the human mind and the possibility of the human tongue.

It was not possible to communicate it by any human means. One had "solely to accept it from God" and "believe." This is how Mary believed.

THE PROMISE OF FAITH IS FULFILLED IN MARY

JOSEPH was unaware of the mystery of Mary, so he suffered very much interiorly. We read: "Joseph her husband, an upright man unwilling to expose her to reproach, decided to send her away quietly" (Mt 1:19).

But a certain night came, when even Joseph "believed." God's Word was addressed to him, and the mystery of Mary, his spouse and consort, became clear to him.

He believed that in her the promise of faith made to Abraham and the prophecy that King David had heard (both Joseph and Mary were from the line of David) were fulfilled.

"Joseph, son of David, do not be afraid to take Mary as your wife, because what is conceived in her is from the Holy Spirit. She is to have a Son, and you are to name Him Jesus because He will save His people from their sins" (Mt 1:20-21).

THE VIRGINAL MYSTERY OF JOSEPH

AGAINST all the expectations of the Old Testament tradition, Christ was born of Mary, who at the moment of the Annunciation clearly declared: "How shall this happen since I do not know man?" (Lk 1:34), thus professing her virginity.

It is true that Christ is born of her like every other human, like any son of his mother. It is also true that His coming into the world is accompanied by the presence of a man who is the spouse of Mary and, in the eyes of the Law and human beings, her husband. Nevertheless, Mary's motherhood is virginal.

And corresponding to this virginal motherhood of Mary is the virginal mystery of Joseph, who following a voice from on high had no fear about taking Mary "as his wife" for what was conceived in her was from the Holy Spirit (cf. Mt 1:20).

"WHAT IS CONCEIVED IN HER IS BY THE HOLY SPIRIT"

IT is true that "Christ's virginal conception and His birth into the world" were hidden from human beings. It is also true that in the eyes of His compatriots of Nazareth He was regarded as "the carpenter's Son" ("ut putabatur filius Joseph"— "thought to be the Son of Joseph": Lk 3:23). Nonetheless, the very reality and essential truth of His conception and birth are far removed from everything that in the Old Testament was exclusively in favor of marriage and rendered celibacy incomprehensible and socially out of favor.

How then could "celibacy for the Kingdom of Heaven" be comprehensible if the expected Messiah must be a "descendant of David" and, as was thought, of royal lineage "according to the flesh"?

Only Mary and Joseph, who lived the mystery of His conception and birth, became the first witnesses of a different fecundity from that of the flesh, that is, the fecundity of the Spirit: "What is conceived in her is from the Holy Spirit" (Mt 1:20).

MARRIAGE OF MARY AND JOSEPH

THE story of Christ's birth is in line with the revelation of that "celibacy for the Kingdom of Heaven" which Christ would one day speak about to His disciples.

However, this fact remained hidden from the people of His time and even from the disciples. Only gradually was it made known to the eyes of the Church on the basis of the testimonies and texts of the Gospels of Matthew and Luke.

"The marriage of Mary and Joseph" (in which the Church honors Joseph as the spouse of Mary and Mary as his spouse) "conceals in itself," at the same time, "the mystery" of the perfect communion of persons, of Man and Woman in the conjugal pact, as well as the mystery of that singular "celibacy for the Kingdom of Heaven": a celibacy that served, in the History of Salvation, the most perfect "fecundity of the Holy Spirit."

CELIBACY FOR THE KINGDOM OF HEAVEN

THIS celibacy will be in a certain sense the absolute fullness of this fecundity, since it is precisely in the conditions at Nazareth, including the pact of Mary and Joseph with reference to marriage and celibacy, that the gift of the incarnation of the Eternal Word was realized. The Son of God, consubstantial with the Father, was conceived and was born like a Man from the Virgin Mary.

The grace of the Hypostatic Union is connected precisely with this, one might say, absolute fullness of supernatural fecundity, a fecundity in the Holy Spirit, which is participated in by a human creature, Mary, on the order of "celibacy for the Kingdom of Heaven."

Mary's Divine Motherhood is also, in a certain sense, a superabundant revelation of that fecundity in the Holy Spirit to which human beings subject their spirit when they freely choose celibacy "in the body": precisely celibacy "for the Kingdom of Heaven."

THE VIRGIN'S DIVINE MOTHERHOOD

THIS image had to be revealed to the consciousness of the Church only gradually in the ever new generations of confessors of Christ when—

together with the Gospel of the Infancy—certainty arose concerning the Divine Motherhood of the Virgin, who had conceived by the power of the Holy Spirit.

Although only in an indirect—yet essential and fundamental—manner, this certainty was to aid the understanding of the sanctity of marriage on the one hand and on the other the disinterest in marriage in view of the "Kingdom of Heaven" of which Christ spoke to His disciples.

THE FEAST OF THE ANNUNCIATION

BEHOLD, I come to do Your will, O My God (cf. Ps 40:8ff; Heb 10:7)

Behold, I am the servant of the Lord (Lk 1:38).

These are the words respectively of the Word Who comes into the world and of Mary who receives the announcement of this event.

It is with these words that I salute this most solemn day that the Liturgy consecrates to the Annunciation of the Lord.

This is a very ancient feast. Although scholars have not yet been able to establish its chronology with certitude, we know that already in the seventh century it was assigned to March 25 (and this assignment must have begun much earlier), because according to a very ancient belief this was the date of the creation of the world and of the death of the Redeemer as well. Indeed, the date assigned to the feast of the Annunciation contributed to the establishment of the date for the feast of Christmas.

Therefore, the solemn feast of this day has great significance, both Marian and chronological.

MARY GIVES HER CONSENT TO THE ANGEL

MARY gives her consent to the Angel of the Annunciation.

The passage from Luke, although very concise, is extremely rich in its Biblical content from the Old Testament and in the unprecedented newness of the Christian revelation: its protagonist is a woman, the Woman beyond compare (cf. Jn 2:4), chosen from all eternity to be the first indispensable collaborator in the Divine plan of salvation.

She is the "almah" prophesied by Isaiah (7:14), the young woman of royal blood who answers to the name of Miriam, of Mary of Nazareth, a lowly and hidden town of Galilee (cf. Jn 1:46). The true Christian "newness" that has elevated women to a lofty and incomparable dignity—inconceivable to the Hebrew mentality of the time as well as to the Greco-Roman civilization—began with this announcement made to Mary by Gabriel in the name of God Himself.

"REJOICE"

MARY is greeted with such sublime words that they frighten her: " 'Kaire, Ave,' Rejoice."

The Messianic joy resounds on earth for the first time. " 'Kecharitomene, gratia plena,' Full of grace."

The Immaculata is here delineated in her mysterious fullness of Divine election, eternal predestination, and luminous clarity. " 'Dominus tecum,' The Lord is with you."

God is with Mary, member of the human family chosen to be the Mother of Emmanuel, of the One Who is "God-with-us." From now on and forever, without regret and without retraction God will be united with humankind, made one with it to save it and grant it His Son, the Redeemer. And Mary is the living, concrete guarantee of this salvific presence of God.

"THE HOLY SPIRIT WILL COME UPON YOU"

THE dialogue between the chosen creature and the Angel of God continues to give rise to other fundamental truths: "You shall conceive and bear a Son, and you shall give Him the Name Jesus. He will be great and will be called Son of the Most High. The Lord God will give Him the throne of David forever. . . . The Holy Spirit will come upon you and the power of the Most High will overshadow you; hence, the holy Offspring to be born will be called the Son of God" (Lk 1:31f, 35).

The Person is coming Who from the line of Adam will enter the genealogies of Abraham and David.

He is "in the line of the Divine promises," but He comes into the world without having need of the trajectory of human paternity, and He even surpasses it in the line of immaculate faith.

The whole Trinity is involved in this work, as the Angel declares: Jesus, the Savior, is the "Son of the Most High," the "Son of God"; the Father is present to extend His shadow over Mary; and the Holy Spirit is present to come down upon her and render her intact womb fruitful by His power.

MARY'S CONSENT

THE Angel asks for Mary's consent so that the Word may come into the world. The expectation of the past centuries is concentrated on this point; on it depends the salvation of the human race.

Commenting on the Annunciation, St. Bernard expresses this unique moment in stupendous fashion when he turns to Our Lady and says: "Prostrate at your feet, the whole world is expectant. And with good reason, because on your lips depends the consolation of the afflicted, the redemption of the imprisoned, the liberation of the condemned, and finally the salvation of all the children of Adam, his whole posterity. Make haste, O Virgin, and respond."

And Mary's consent is one of faith. It is found in the line of faith. Justly, then, has the Second Vatican Council, in reflecting on Mary as prototype and model of the Church, proposed her as an example of active faith precisely at the moment of her "fiat" (let it be done): "Mary was not merely a passive instrument in God's hands, but . . . she cooperated in the salvation of the human race with willing faith and obedience" (LG 56).

HERE I AM!

"THE Annunciation invites us to follow the steps of Mary's active faith": "a willing faith," which opens itself to the Word of God, which assists the will of God, whatever it be and however it is manifested; "a strong faith," which overcomes all difficulties, incomprehensions, and crises; "an operative faith," nourished as a living flame of love, which desires to cooperate strongly with the plan of God for us.

"Behold, I am the servant of the Lord": each of us, as the Council invites, must be ready to respond this way, like her, in faith and obedience, to cooperate each in our own sphere of responsibility, in building up the Kingdom of God.

Mary's response was the perfect echo of the response of the Word to the Father. The "Behold" of the Virgin is possible insofar as it was preceded and sustained by the "Behold" of the Son of God, Who at the moment of Mary's consent becomes the Son of Man.

SEASON OF LENT

114

ANNUNCIATION = VOCATION

ANNUNCIATION signifies vocation: this is the
day on which the Virgin of Nazareth received
the revelation of her exceptional vocation; the day
on which the Virgin of Nazareth, having learned her
own vocation, gave a brief response: "Behold, I am
the servant of the Lord."

The mystery of the Annunciation has its continuity; even though it is unique, it always has its
analogies in the life of the Church because the life of
the Church is constituted by the intermediary of vocations, diverse vocations.

The Christian life is a vocation that can be
likened to the vocation of the Virgin of Nazareth.

GOD CALLS

WE have contemplated the Annunciation and
we have contemplated at the same time
another Divine and human mystery: the mystery of
a vocation.

This mystery of a vocation is deeply imbedded in
the contemplation of the Annunciation because in a
vocation it is always God Who calls and human beings who are called, and in the Annunciation it is
God Who calls and the Virgin of Nazareth who is
called.

We can unearth the various elements of a vocation. They are such and such! But some are characteristic, typical in a special way, and we find them
in the content of the Annunciation.

"DO NOT BE AFRAID"

"DO not be afraid." This is the constitutive element of a vocation—because human beings are afraid. Not only are they afraid of being called to the priesthood but they are also afraid of being called to life, to its duties, to a profession, to marriage. They are afraid. This fear also reveals a sense of responsibility, but not a mature responsibility.

We must overcome this fear in order to arrive at mature responsibility. We must accept the call, we must listen, we must receive, we must measure our efforts and respond: Yes, Yes!

Do not be afraid, do not fear because you have found Grace. Do not fear life, do not fear motherhood, do not fear your marriage, do not fear your priesthood—because you have found Grace.

THE EARTH AWAITS YOUR "YES"

THIS certainty and this consciousness aid us as they aided Mary. Behold: "The earth and paradise await your 'Yes,' O most pure Virgin." These are the words of St. Bernard, celebrated and marvelous words.

They await your "Yes," O Mary. They await your "Yes," O mother who are about to give birth. They await your "Yes," O you who are about to assume your personal, familial, and social responsibility. They await your "Yes," O you who are called to be a priest. Your "Yes."

This "Yes" becomes mature as the fruit of a union of two factors: Grace (you have found Grace) and your efforts (I am ready to collaborate, I am ready to give myself).

This is Mary's response; this is the response of a mother; this is the response of a young person: a "Yes" that lasts for one's whole life. Today people are afraid to make a response that binds for life, not only in the priesthood but also in marriage.

And yet the "Yes" for a lifetime is the measure of a human being.

First of all, it is the criterion of one's dignity as a person. Secondly, it is the measure of one's strengths and efforts. Fidelity is required to carry out the "Yes" for a lifetime.

THE FEAST OF THE ANNUNCIATION

"THE Annunciation of the Lord." This is a feast that has always possessed special relevance in the liturgical calendar because of the great mystery of mercy and love that it contains and expresses: the mystery of the very Son of God Who became Son of Man and was made flesh in the most pure womb of the Virgin Mary.

Jesus Christ—it is important to remember—is the protagonist, "always" the unique and true protagonist, in the whole work of human Redemption.

He is such from the first moment, which is the specific moment of the Incarnation, when "immediately after" the Annunciation the Angel made to Mary and "as a consquence" of her consent to what he announced "the Word became flesh and made His dwelling among us" (Jn 1:14).

THE CONTENT OF THE ANNOUNCEMENT

THERE in the land of Galilee, in the modest home of Nazareth, in addition to the Archangel Gabriel "who brings the announcement (subject) and Mary "who receives the announcement" (terminus) is the One Who needs to be seen with the eyes of faith: it is He Who constitutes the "content of the announcement" (object).

Hence, we will invoke and bless the Angel of the announcement. We will invoke in particular and bless Mary, calling her and venerating her with the title of "Virgin of the Annunciation," which is so dear to popular piety.

But in the center of these two personages, we must always distinguish, invoke, bless, and adore the announced Son of God as the most august Host Who is present and active.

ANNOUNCEMENT OF INEFFABLE JOY

"DO NOT be afraid, Mary. You shall conceive and bear a Son, and you shall give Him the Name Jesus. He will be great and will be called Son of the Most High . . ." (Lk 1:30-31). This, in sum-mary, in the stark simplicity of the Gospel language, is the announcement: the conception and virginal birth of the very Son of God.

This announcement was first made by the Angel to Mary, then it was communicated to Joseph her future husband (cf. Mt 1:20f), and finally it was transmitted to the shepherds and the Magi (cf. Lk 2:10-11; Mt 2:2ff). The One Who is announced and is about to be born, or has just been born, is the "Savior," and in precise accord with what His Name signifies "He will save His people from their sins" (Mt 1:21).

In the theological perspective of salvation, this announcement is addressed to "all" humankind throughout the centuries, as an announcement of ineffable joy.

BLESSED BECAUSE OF MOTHERHOOD

THE mystery of the Incarnation is a grand and sublime mystery, which our feeble intelligence cannot truly comprehend because it is incapable of grasping the reasons for God's "actions." In it we must always see, in a position of primary evidence, Jesus Christ, as the Son of God, Who becomes flesh, and beside Him the one who cooperated in the Incarnation, giving Him her very flesh with the love of a mother.

In this way, the Annunciation of the Lord detracts nothing from the function and merit of Mary, who "precisely because of her Motherhood" will be, together with her Divine Son, blessed for all ages.

MARY AT CALVARY

WE must always see the mystery of the Incarnation not detached from but connected with all the mysteries of the Hidden Life and Public Life of Jesus up to the other and sublime mystery of the Redemption. From Nazareth to Calvary there is a line of ordered development, in the continuation of an undivided and indivisible design of love.

This is why on Calvary we will reencounter Mary, who shows herself as truly a Mother watching and praying at the foot of the Cross of her dying Son and as "associated" with Him, that is, as cooperating in His salvific work: "In subordination to Him and along with Him, by the grace of Almighty God, she served the mystery of the Redemption" (LG 56).

THE ANNUNCIATION INAUGURATES THE REDEMPTION

IN the Annunciation the beginning of the Redemption of the world took place: Emmanuel, God-with-us, "is that Christ" Who in the Letter to the Hebrews "speaks" to the Father: "Sacrifice and oblation You did not desire, but a body You have prepared for Me. Holocausts and sin offerings You took no delight in. Then I said, 'Behold, I come . . . to do, O God, Your will' " (Heb 10:5-7).

Thus says Christ, Eternal Word of the Father, and His beloved Son. In these words lies the beginning of the Redemption of the world and His entire plan to its very end.

The Redemption of the world is connected with the "Body received from Mary and offered in the sacrifice of the Cross," which then became the Body of the resurrection: of the "firstborn from the dead" (Rv 1:5).

DOOR OF ENTRY FOR THE REDEEMER

IN its very beginnings the Redemption of the world is connected with a word that makes Christ's admirable obedience resound in the holy "obedience of the Virgin of Nazareth." It is to her that Gabriel's announcement is directed. And it is she who hears the Angel's decisive response to her principal question: "The Holy Spirit will come upon you and the power of the Most High will overshadow you; hence, the holy Offspring to be born will be called the Son of God" (Lk 1:35).

And it is precisely she, Mary of Nazareth, who "accepts" this response, and welcomes into her womb and into her heart the Son of God as Son of Man. And in her "the Word became flesh," after this word of obedience that echoes Christ's: "Behold, I am the servant of the Lord. Let it be done to me as you say" (Lk 1:38).

Out of her, the first among the redeemed, God fashioned a door of entry for the Redeemer of the world.

REJOICE, JERUSALEM!

"REJOICE, JERUSALEM; and all you who love her, come together!" During Lent, I love to see that the Liturgy, through the words of Isaiah, applies to the Church the mystery of the Virgin Mary, of her joy and her motherly sorrow.

For Mary is the true Daughter of Zion, spiritual recapitulation of the ancient Jerusalem, beginning and summit of the Church of Christ. Even more, she is the new Eve, the true mother of all the living.

As the Daughter of Zion and the new Eve, she is invited to rejoice. Human sorrow can be understood only in the context of a lost happiness; and sorrow has meaning only in the light of a happiness promised. "Rejoice, Jerusalem!"

SHE SUFFERED FOR US

THE suffering of Jerusalem spoken of by the Prophets was the consequence of the infidelity of her children, who had provoked punishment from God and exile from their homeland.

The suffering of this mysterious new Daughter of Zion, Mary, is the consequence of the countless faults of all the children of Adam, faults that caused our expulsion from paradise.

Hence, in Mary the salvific mystery of suffering and the significance and amplitude of human solidarity are revealed in a unique way.

For the Blessed Virgin did not suffer for herself, being the All-Beautiful One and the ever Immaculate One. She suffered for us, insofar as she is the Mother of us all.

THE ROYAL ROAD OF RECONCILIATION

JUST as Christ "bore our infirmities and endured our sufferings" (Is 53:4), so also Mary was burdened as though by pains of childbirth in attaining a vast motherhood that will regenerate us for God.

The suffering of Mary, the New Eve, alongside the New Adam, Christ, was and remains the royal road of the reconciliation of the world: "Rejoice, Jerusalem! And all you who love her rejoice with her!" (cf. Is 66:10).

In the person of the Virgin Mary, marked by suffering because of the infidelity of her children but invited to exult with joy because of their redemption, our suffering is also situated. We too can become "a particle of the infinite treasure of the Redemption of the world," so that others can share this treasure and reach the fullness of joy that it has merited for us.

THE DISCIPLE TOOK HER INTO HIS HOME

THE words that, from the height of the Cross, Jesus addressed respectively to His Mother and to the disciple whom He loved entrust them to each other in an exchange of maternal and filial relationships (cf. Jn 19:26f).

The evangelical text just cited offers us a model of Marian devotion. "From that hour onward, the disciple took her into his home" (Jn 19:27).

Can the same thing be said of us? Do we also take Mary into our home? We should welcome her with full title into the home of our life, our faith, our affections, and our commitments. We should acknowledge the motherly role that is proper to her—as dispenser of guidance, advice and exhortation, or simply as a silent presence, which at times is enough to infuse strength and courage into us.

MARY, MOTHER OF ALL

FROM the moment when Jesus, dying on the Cross, said to John: "There is your Mother"; from the moment when "the disciple took her into his home," the mystery of the "spiritual Motherhood" of Mary had its fulfillment in history with an amplitude that has no limits.

Motherhood signifies solicitude for the life of a child. Now if Mary is the Mother of all human beings, her concern for the life of each is "universal in scope." A mother's concern embraces the whole person.

Mary's Motherhood has its beginnings in her maternal care for Christ. In Christ she accepted John at the foot of the Cross and in Him "she has accepted every person and the whole person." Mary embraces everyone with a special solicitude "in the Holy Spirit."

"WOMAN, THERE IS YOUR SON"

" JESUS said to His Mother, 'Woman, there is your son.' In turn He said to the disciple, 'There is your Mother' " (Jn 19:26f).

The circumstances in which this Motherhood of Mary was proclaimed show the importance that the Redeemer attached to it.

At the very moment when Jesus was consummating His sacrifice, He said to His Mother those basic words: "Woman, there is your son," and to the disciple: "There is your Mother" (Jn 19:26f). And the Evangelist remarks that after pronouncing them Jesus was aware that everything had been accomplished.

The giving of His Mother was the final gift that He was bestowing on humankind as the fruit of His sacrifice.

It is therefore a question of an action that wishes to crown the work of redemption.

By asking Mary to treat the beloved disciple as her son, Jesus invites her to accept the sacrifice of His Death and, as the price of such acceptance, to assume a new Motherhood.

THE SIGN OF A SPECIAL LOVE

A S the Savior of all humankind, Christ wishes to give Mary's Motherhood its widest extension.

Therefore, He chooses John as the symbol of all the disciples and He indicates that the gift of His Mother is the sign of a special intention of love, with which He embraces all those whom He wishes to draw to Himself as disciples, that is, all Christians and all people.

Moreover, by giving this Motherhood an individual form Jesus manifests His will to make of Mary not only the Mother of His disciples as a whole but also of each one of them in particular, as if each were her only child in place of her unique Son.

SINGULAR PARTICIPATION IN THE MEDIATION OF CHRIST

T HE Motherhood of Mary in the order of grace "continues without interruption" until the end of the world, declares the Council, and it stresses in particular the help that the Blessed Virgin showers on the brothers and sisters of her Son in their dangers and trials (cf. LG 62).

Mary's mediation constitutes a singular participation in the unique mediation of Christ, which for this reason is in no way overshadowed by it. On the contrary, Christ's mediation remains the central fact in the work of salvation.

MARY'S COOPERATION IN HER SON'S WORK

THIS universal Motherhood, in the spiritual order, was the ultimate consequence of Mary's cooperation in the work of her Divine Son, a cooperation that began in the trembling joy of the Annunciation and that developed into the infinite sorrow of Calvary. This is what the Second Vatican Council emphasized when it specified the role to which Mary has been destined in the Church:

"Mary conceived, brought forth, and nourished Christ. She presented Him to the Father in the Temple and was with Him in suffering as He died on the Cross. In an utterly singular way, she cooperated by her obedience, faith, hope, and burning charity in the Savior's work of restoring supernatural life to souls. For this reason she is a Mother to us in the order of grace" (LG 61).

WITNESS OF FILIAL AFFECTION

DEVOTION to Our Lady is not opposed to devotion to her Son. On the contrary, we can say that by asking the beloved disciple to treat Mary as his Mother, Jesus established the cult of Mary.

John made haste to carry out the will of his Master: from that moment onward he took Mary into his home, and he accorded her a filial affection that corresponded to the motherly affection of the Blessed Virgin toward him. In this way he inaugurated a relationship of spiritual intimacy that contributed to deepen the relation John had with the Master, whose unique traits he discovered on the countenance of the Mother.

Thus, the Marian movement was born on Calvary and continues to grow unceasingly in the Christian community.

TO GATHER INTO ONE THE DISPERSED CHILDREN

THE words that the Crucified Christ addressed to His Mother and to the beloved disciple have brought a new dimension to the religious condition of human beings. The presence of a Mother in the life of grace is a source of consolation and joy.

In the motherly countenance of Mary, Christians perceive a most singular expression of the merciful love of God, Who through the mediaton of a motherly presence makes us better understand His solicitude and goodness as a Father.

Mary appears as the one who draws sinners and reveals to them—with her sympathy and her indulgence—the Divine offering of reconciliation.

THE VALUE OF MARY'S MOTHERHOOD

MARY'S Motherhood is not only individual. It has a collective value that is expressed in the title "Mother of the Church." For she united herself on Calvary with the sacrifice of her Son that effected the formation of the Church; her motherly heart shares most deeply in the will of Christ "to gather into one all the dispersed children of God" (Jn 11:52).

In suffering for the Church, Mary merited to become the Mother of all the disciples of her Son, the Mother of their unity. That is why the Council declares that "taught by the Holy Spirit, the Catholic Church honors her with filial affection and piety as a most beloved Mother" (LG 53).

MOTHER OF UNITY

THE Church regards Mary as a Mother who watches over the Church's development and never ceases to intercede with her Son to obtain for Christians the most profound sentiments of faith, hope, and love.

Mary seeks to foster as much as possible the unity of Christians, because a Mother strives to insure harmony among her children. There is no heart more ecumenical or more ardent than the heart of Mary.

It is to this perfect Mother that the Church has recourse in all her difficulties. It is to her that the Church entrusts her projects, because she knows that in praying to and loving Mary she is responding to the desire the Savior manifested on the Cross and she is certain that she will not be deceived in her invocations.

THE CREATURE WITH A "NEW HEART"

IN Lent, which calls us to a renewed path to conversion, our gaze turns to Mary, perfect image of the Church. In her indeed we contemplate the creature with a new heart, the attentive and concerned Woman, the disciple who knows how to listen and pray without ceasing, the Virgin of the silent sacrifice.

Mary is the creature with the "new heart," announced by the Prophets. God had promised such a one: "I will give you a new heart and place a new spirit within you" (Ez 36:26).

Mary's historical development, beginning with the Immaculate Conception, took place completely under the shadow of the Spirit. But it was especially at the Annunciation that she received from the Holy Spirit the "new heart" that rendered her docile to God, capable of welcoming His plan of salvation and corresponding to it with absolute fidelity for her whole life.

She is the "faithful Virgin": the one who epitomizes the ancient Israel and prefigures the Church, wedded to God forever in faithfulness and love (cf. Hos 2:21f).

THE WOMAN ATTENTIVE TO THE NEEDS OF OTHERS

MARY is the Woman attentive to and concerned for the spiritual and material needs of her brothers and sisters. The Gospel highlights her solicitude for the aged Elizabeth, her discreet intervention at the wedding feast of Cana to the joy of the young couple, and her motherly welcome for the disciple and all the redeemed at the foot of the Cross. We are certain that from heaven she continues to prolong her mediation on behalf of all of us, poor exiled children of Eve.

In addition, Mary is a disciple who has incarnated the Gospel even to the extent of sacrifice and the martyrdom by an unbloody "sword" that Simeon had prophesied to her in the Temple, uniting her destiny with the bloody sacrifice of her Son.

In the face of the disconcerting proposal of God to her, she never hesitated to repeat every day her "Yes" of the Annunciation, so that it could become the "Yes" of Easter, for herself and for the whole human race.

THE GOSPEL OF SUFFERING

A BOVE all else, it is consoling—and this accords with the evangelical and historical truth—to note that alongside Christ, in the very first place next to Him and completely visible, there is always His most holy Mother. "By her whole life" she renders an exemplary testimony to this particular Gospel of suffering.

In Mary the countless and intense sufferings accumulated with such cohesiveness and such concatenation that while showing her unshakable faith they also contributed to the redemption of all.

In reality, beginning from her secret conversation with the Angel, Mary understood that her mission of Mother "destined" her to share the very mission of her Son in an absolutely unique manner. And she soon had a confirmation of this point by the events that accompanied the birth of Jesus at Bethlehem, by the formal announcement made by the aged Simeon who spoke of a sharp sword that was to pierce her heart, or by the anguish and privation generated in the precipitous flight to Egypt, provoked by the cruel decision of Herod.

AT THE FOOT OF THE CROSS

U NDOUBTEDLY, Mary participated with acute sensitivity in her Son's hidden and public life.

However, it was on Calvary that the sufferings of Mary most holy, alongside the sufferings of Jesus, reached a height difficult to imagine from the human point of view but certainly one that was mysterious and supernaturally fruitful for the purposes of universal salvation.

Mary's ascent to Calvary and her "presence" at the foot of the Cross together with the beloved disciple constituted a most special participation in the redemptive Death of her Son. In like manner, the words that she heard from His lips represented as it were a solemn handing over of this particular Gospel, destined to be announced to the whole community of believers.

WITNESS OF CHRIST'S PASSION

A WITNESS of the Passion of her Son by her "presence" and a "participant" in it by her "compassion," Mary most holy offered a singular contribution to the Gospel of suffering, confirming in advance the words of Paul (cf. Col 1:24). Truly indeed, she had very special reasons for being able to assert that she "completes in her body"—as already in her heart as well—"what is lacking in the sufferings of Christ."

In the light of Christ's incomparable example, which is reflected with singular evidence in the life of His Mother, the Gospel of suffering becomes, through the experience and the word of the Apostles, the "inexhaustible source for the ever new generations" that succeed one another in the history of the Church.

A NEW MOTHERHOOD

TO His suffering brothers and sisters, Christ "opens up" and displays in gradual fashion "the horizons of the Kingdom of God": a world connected with its Creator, a world free from sin and being built up on the saving power of love.

And slowly but efficaciously, Christ introduces those who suffer into this world, into this Kingdom of the Father—and He does so in a sense through the very heart of their suffering!

Suffering cannot be "transformed" and changed by a grace from outside, but only by an "inner" grace. By His own salvific suffering Christ finds Himself at the most profound point of any human suffering and can work within it by the power of His Spirit of truth, of His Consoler Spirit.

This is not all. The Divine Redeemer wishes to penetrate into the soul of every person who suffers—with the aid of the heart of His most holy Mother, firstfruits and summit of all the redeemed.

As if in continuation of the Motherhood that through the working of the Holy Spirit had given

Him life, Christ at the moment of His Death conferred on Mary ever Virgin "a new Motherhood"— a spiritual and universal Motherhood—in regard to all human beings. He did this to help everyone in the pilgrimage of faith remain closely united to Him in the company of Mary unto the Cross and by the power of this Cross to transform every suffering from human weakness into the power of God.

YOU HAVE PRAYED FOR THE CHURCH

WE greet you,
    Mother of our Lord Jesus Christ.
When Jesus on the Cross saw you,
He said to you regarding John:
"Woman, there is your son" (Jn 19:26).
"With the Apostles,"
with the women and the brothers
united in prayer,
you prayed for the Church
and implored the gift of the Holy Spirit.

This Spirit has given to the Apostles
and to all the messengers of the faith
the power to carry out the mandate
that the Lord had entrusted to them:
"Go therefore and make disciples
of all the nations" (Mt 28:19).

MARY'S FAITHFUL OBEDIENCE

BLESSED Virgin Mary,
most humble servant of the Lord!
By your faithful obedience
and your fidelity to Christ,
by your steadfast devotion
and motherly love,
you are the "model of the Church" (LG 63),
that has been saved
and filled with graces for us
by God through Your Son.

"At the same time,"
you yourself are "its most chosen member,"
and you remained amidst the Apostles who,
on the day of the descent of the Spirit,
received the mandate
to lead the people
from "every nation under heaven" (Acts 2:5)—
by preaching—
to conversion and Baptism,
and to increase the community of believers
(Acts 2:14, 38, 41).

HELP US TO LIVE THE GOSPEL WITH THE "FOLLY" OF THE CROSS

O MOTHER of mercy,
we entrust to your loving heart
the entire people and Church of this land.

Keep us from all injustice,
division, violence, and war.

Protect us from temptation
and the slavery of sin and evil.

Be with us!

Help us to overcome doubt by faith,
egoism by service,
pride by meekness,
and hatred by love.

Help us to live the Gospel
with the "folly" of the Cross,
giving testimony to Christ
Who died on it,
so that we may rise with your Son
to the true life with the Father
in the unity of the Holy Spirit.

O Mother of Christ,
comfort and strengthen
all those who suffer:
the poor,
the lonely,
the rich,
the unloved,
the oppressed,
and the forgotten.

Bless us!

Pray for us,
with St. Joseph,
and unite us in love.

Grant peace to our divided earth
and the light of hope to all.

Show us the blessed fruit of your womb,
Jesus!

SEASON OF EASTER

TEACH US THE ATTITUDES
OF THE GOOD SHEPHERD

TEACH us and grant us the attitudes
of the Good Shepherd.

Nourish and increase
our apostolic dedication.

Fortify and regenerate without ceasing our love
for those who suffer.

Illumine and stimulate
our promise of virginity
for the Kingdom of Heaven.

Infuse and keep in us
the sense of fraternity and of communion.

With our lives
we entrust to you, dear Mother,
the lives of our parents and family members
and those of our brothers and sisters.

May your motherly attentions
always precede our steps
toward them
and constantly direct our path
toward the Homeland
that Christ, your Son and our Lord,
has prepared for us by His Redemption.
Amen.

BELOVED DAUGHTER OF THE FATHER

MARY, we greet you as once Elizabeth greeted you: "Blessed are you among women, and blessed is the fruit of your womb. . . . Blessed is she who has believed that the Lord's words to her would be fulfilled" (Lk 1:42).

We greet you, beloved Daughter of the Heavenly Father, Mother of the Son of God, and Sanctuary of the Holy Spirit. "You have found grace with God." The Holy Spirit has come upon you and the Most High has cast the shadow of His power over you (cf. Lk 1:30, 35).

THE SALVIFIC WILL OF GOD

YOU are the "woman" from whom "was born the Savior" (Gal 4:4), the One Whom God has established as "the firstborn of many brothers and sisters" (Rom 8:29), to Whom you are close by motherly love.

We greet you, Daughter of Zion, you who have trod the path "of the pilgrimage of faith" (LG 58) from the moment when you remained standing at the foot of the Cross and in this way was accomplished God's salvific will, to which you gave your wholehearted assent.

As the Mother of Compassion, you suffered with your Son when He offered Himself once and for all to His Father for us (cf. Heb 7:27).

A MOTHER'S RIGHT

WITH her Easter antiphon "Regina Caeli" (Queen of Heaven), the Church speaks to the Mother, the one who had the good fortune to bear in her womb, next to her heart, and later in her arms, the Son of God and our Savior.

The last time she received Him in her arms was on Calvary, when He was taken down from the Cross. Under her eyes He was wrapped in the funeral shroud and taken to the sepulcher. Under the very eyes of His Mother!

Then on the third day the tomb was found empty. But Mary was not the first one to discover this fact. First there were the "three Marys," and among them especially Mary Magdalene, the converted sinner. A little later the Apostles also discovered this fact after being notified by the women.

And even though the Gospels tell us nothing about a visit of Christ's Mother to the place of His Resurrection, all of us still think: "She must have been the first one there in some way." She must have been the first to "share in the mystery of the Resurrection," because it was a Mother's right for her to do so.

ALL-POWERFUL INTERCESSION

THE Liturgy of the Church respects this Mother's right of Mary when it directs to her this special invitation to the joy of the Resurrection: "Rejoice and be glad! He has risen as He said!" And this same antiphon joins to the invitation a request for Mary's intercession: "Pray for us to God!"

The revelation of the Divine power of the Son through the Resurrection is at the same time the revelation of Mary's "all-powerful intercession" ("omnia potentia supplex") with her Son.

The Church of all ages, beginning with the Upper Room of Pentecost, has surrounded Mary with a special veneration and has addressed her with a particular confidence.

A MOTHERLY PRESENCE

"THE Church of our time" has made, through the voice of the Second Vatican Council, a synthesis of all the Marian developments throughout the centuries.

Chapter eight of the Constitution "Lumen Gentium" ("The Light of Nations") is in a certain sense the "magna charta" of Mariology for our age: Mary present in a special way in the mystery of the Church, "Mother of the Church," as Pope Paul VI began calling her (in the Credo for the People of God), dedicating to her a special document entitled "Marialis Cultus" (Devotion to Mary).

This presence of Mary in the mystery of the Church, and at the same time in the daily life of the People of God throughout the world, "is above all a Motherly presence."

THE FULFILLMENT
OF THE SALVIFIC MYSTERY

MARY, so to speak, endows the salvific work of her Son and the mission of the Church with a singular form: the maternal form. All that human language can say on the subject of the "genius" proper to woman-mother—the genius of the heart—is referred entirely to her.

Mary is ever the most complete "fulfillment" of the salvific mystery—from the Immaculate Conception to the Assumption—and she is continually the most efficacious announcement of this mystery. She reveals salvation and brings grace even to those who seem the most indifferent and the most distant.

In the world, which side by side with progress also manifests its "corruption" and its "aging," Mary never ceases being "the beginning of a better world," as Paul VI expressed it.

BRINGING YOUNG PEOPLE TO MARY

"THE Blessed Virgin Mary," writes the late Pontiff Paul VI, "offers a calm vision and a reassuring word to people today: . . . the victory of hope over anguish, of fellowship over solitude, of peace over anxiety, of joy and beauty over boredom and disgust . . . of life over death" (MC 57).

I wish to bring the young people of the whole world and of the entire Church to Mary, who is the Mother of true Love. She bears within her an indestructible sign of youth and beauty that never fade away.

THE FULLEST EXPRESSION OF FIDELITY TO THE SPIRIT

I WISH and pray that young people go to Mary, that they have faith in her, entrust to her the lives they have before them, and love her with a simple and burning love from their hearts. She alone is able to respond to this love in the best way.

"Mary alone is a living incarnation" of the total and complete dedication to God, to Christ, and to His salvific action that must find its adequate expression in every priestly and religious vocation.

Mary is the fullest expression of perfect fidelity to the Holy Spirit and His action in the soul. She is the expression of the fidelity that signifies a persevering cooperation with the grace of a vocation.

THE UNDERSTANDING OF MYSTERIES

THE Gospels do not speak of an appearance of the Risen Jesus to His Mother. This ineffable mystery of joy remains beneath the veil of a mystical silence.

Nevertheless, it is certain that just as Mary, the first among the redeemed, was especially close to the Cross of her Son, so she also had a privileged experience of the Risen One. And this experience inspired in her a most intense joy, a joy unique among all the creatures saved by the Blood of Christ.

Mary is our guide in the understanding of the mysteries of the Lord. Just as in her and with her we comprehend the meaning of the Cross, so in her and with her we succeed in grasping the meaning of the Resurrection and in knowing the joy that emanates from this experience.

CAUSE OF OUR JOY

MARY is the only one among all creatures who "believed" right from the start in everything that the Word, becoming incarnate in her, accomplished in the world, for the salvation of the world.

In a transport of exultation founded on faith, her joy has passed from that of the "Magnificat," full of hope, to that most pure joy without the slightest shadow of decline, because of her Son's triumph over sin and death.

Mary is the one who "cooperated," as the Second Vatican Council describes her, "by her obedience, faith, hope, and ardent charity in the Savior's work of restoring supernatural life to souls" (LG 61).

QUEEN OF HEAVEN

MARY "cares for her Son's brothers and sisters who still sojourn on earth surrounded by dangers and difficulties, until they are led to their happy Homeland" (LG 62).

May Mary's path be also our own. May her joy be also our own. And just as she, joyous over the Resurrection of her Son, is the cause of our joy ("causa nostrae laetitiae"), so let us commit ourselves to be the cause of her joy by allowing Christ the Redeemer to fashion supernatural life in us, until the eternal joy of our happy Homeland. "With her, Queen of Heaven!"

THE MOST PRECIOUS FRUIT

WE wish to consider in Mary what we might term the "success" of the Paschal Mystery: its "accomplishment," its happy outcome. Indeed, the Paschal Mystery, glorification of life, is in space and time the perennial source of life, and when it is lived in imitation of Christ it inevitably bears fruit.

Jesus did not die in vain. His death is like the seed sown in the earth: it is fertile with results. And its most beautiful and most exalted fruit is the glorious triumph of Mary, His Mother.

Mary is the most precious fruit of the seed of eternal life that God, in Jesus Christ, has sown in her heart of a humankind in need of salvation after Adam's sin.

MOST EXALTED "ACCOMPLISHMENT" OF THE PASCHAL MYSTERY

MARY is the most exalted "accomplishment" of the Paschal Mystery; she is the most "accomplished" woman both in the order of nature and in the order of grace. More than any other human creature she knew how to meditate upon, understand, and live this Paschal Mystery.

For the Christian, it is impossible to experience the meaning of Easter by abstracting from the way in which Mary has lived it, with and through Christ, in victory over the ancient adversary.

In the mystery of her assumption into heaven in soul and body the whole Church will celebrate the absolute fulfillment of the Paschal Mystery, because in the Mother of God so glorified the Church sees the ideal type and the terminus of her own journey through the ages.

FOLLOWING MARY'S EXAMPLE

IT IS in Mary and with Mary that we are enabled to penetrate the meaning of the Paschal Mystery, allowing it to bring forth in us the immense riches of its effects and its fruits of eternal life. It is in her and with her that we can do so, since she did not pass from sin to grace, as all of us have done, but through a singular privilege owing to the merits of Christ she was preserved from sin and began journeying toward the eternal Easter from the very first moment of her existence.

Indeed, her whole life was an "Easter," a "Passover"—a passage, a journey of joy—from the joy of hope at the moment of trial to the joy of possession after the triumph over death. Her human person, as we know through a solemn definition of the Church, has in the wake of the Risen One accomplished the Easter passage in soul and body from death to a glorious eternal life.

Following Mary's example, we too are invited to welcome Christ, Who pardons us, redeems us, saves us, and works in us the Easter passage from death to life.

THE MERCY OF MARY

THE Liturgy of the Easter Season places on our lips the words of the Psalm: "The mercies of the Lord I will sing forever" (Ps 89:2).

These Easter words of the Church echo, with the fullness of their prophetic content, the words already uttered by Mary during her visit to Elizabeth, wife of Zechariah: "His mercy is from age to age" (Lk 1:50).

From the moment of the Incarnation, these words open up a new perspective in the History of Salvation. After the Resurrection of Christ, this perspective is now on the historical plane and at the same time on the eschatological plane as well.

From that time ever new generations of people succeed one another in the immense human family in increasing numbers. New generations of People of God also succeed one another, marked with the sign of the Cross and the Resurrection and "sealed" (cf. 2 Cor 1:21f) with the sign of Christ's Paschal Mystery, absolute revelation of the mercy that Mary proclaimed at the threshold of her cousin's house: "His mercy is from age to age" (Lk 1:50).

MARY'S PARTICIPATION
IN THE REVELATION OF MERCY

MARY is also the one who, in a particular and exceptional manner—like no other—experienced mercy and at the same time, always in an exceptional manner, made possible by the sacrifice of her heart her own participation in the revelation of the Divine mercy. Such a sacrifice is closely connected with her Son's Cross at the foot of which she would find herself on Calvary.

Mary's sacrifice is a specific participation in the revelation of mercy, namely, God's absolute fidelity to His love, to His Covenant that He willed from all eternity and that He concluded in time with man, with people, with the human race. It is the participation in that revelation that has been definitively completed through the Cross.

"No one has experienced as much as the Mother of the Crucified" the mystery of the Cross, the disconcerting encounter of the transcendent Divine justice with love: that "kiss" given by mercy to justice (cf. Ps 85:11).

A PROFOUND KNOWLEDGE
OF THE DIVINE MERCY

NO one has like Mary so profoundly and wholeheartedly accepted that mystery: that truly Divine dimension of the Redemption, which was realized on Calvary by the Death of her Son, together with the sacrifice of her heart of a mother, together with her definitive "Yes." Mary is thus the one who "knows most the mystery of the Divine mercy." She knows what it cost and she knows how great it is.

In this sense, we call her also the "Mother of mercy": Our Lady of mercy or Mother of the Divine mercy. In each of these titles there is a profound theological significance, because they express the particular preparation of her soul, of her whole personality, for knowing how to discern—in the complex events of the first Israel and of every person and then the whole of humankind—that mercy in which "from age to age" (Lk 1:50) all share in accord with the eternal plan of the Blessed Trinity.

LEARNING TO LOVE

THE titles we attribute to the Mother of God speak to her above all as the Mother of the Crucified and Risen One; as "the one who having experienced that mercy in an existential way" in equal fashion "merits" "such mercy" throughout her earthly life and especially at the foot of the Cross of her Son; and finally as the one who, through her hidden and at the same time incomparable participation in the Messianic mission of her Son, has been called in a special way to bring to humans that love which He had come to reveal.

This love finds its most concrete expression toward those who suffer, the poor, the imprisoned, the blind, the oppressed, and sinners, as Christ indicated with the words of Isaiah's prophecy, first in the synagogue of Nazareth (cf. Lk 4:18) and later in His response to the messengers from John the Baptist (cf. Lk 7:22).

THE GIFTS THAT ASSURE
OUR ETERNAL SALVATION

A PARTICIPANT in a singular and exceptional way in this "merciful" love of Christ, which is manifested above all in contact with moral and physical evil, was the heart of Mary, Mother of the Crucified and Risen One. And in her and thanks to her this love never ceases to reveal itself in the heart of the Church and of humankind.

Such a revelation is especially fruitful because it is founded, in the Mother of God, on the singular tact of her motherly heart, on her particular sensitivity, on her special capacity to unite all "who more readily accept merciful love from a mother." This is one of the great and vivifying mysteries of Christianity, so closely connected with the mystery of the Incarnation.

"This Motherhood of Mary in the order of grace," as the Second Vatican Council declares, "will last without interruption from the moment of her consent, which she gave in faith at the Annunciation and sustained without wavering beneath the Cross, until the eternal coronation of all the elect. For, taken up to heaven, she did not lay aside this saving role but by her manifold acts of intercession she continues to win for us the graces for eternal life'' (LG 62).

MOTHER OF THE CHURCH

MARY is the Mother of the Church because in virtue of the ineffable election of the Eternal Father Himself (LG 56) and under the special action of the Spirit of love (LG 56) she has given human life to the Son of God, "for Whom and through Whom all things exist" (Heb 2:10) and from Whom the whole People of God receives the grace and dignity of its election. Her own Son willed explicitly to extend the Motherhood of His Mother—in a manner easily accessible to all souls and all hearts—by giving her from the height of the Cross His beloved disciple as a son (cf. Jn 19:26).

The Holy Spirit inspired her to remain, after our Lord's Ascension, in the Upper Room recollected in prayer and expectation in union with the Apostles until the day of Pentecost, on which the Church was to rise from obscurity and be visibly born (cf. Acts 1:14).

Since then, all the generations of disciples and those who confess and love Christ—like John the Apostle—have spiritually taken into their home (cf. Jn 19:27) this Mother, who in this way right from the beginning, namely, the moment of the Annunciation, has been inserted into the History of Salvation and the mission of the Church.

THE GRACE OF DIVINE MOTHERHOOD

ALL of us who form the present generation of Christ's disciples desire to unite ourselves to Mary in a special way. We do so with our whole attachment to ancient tradition and at the same time with full respect and love for the members of all Christian Communities.

We do so under the impulsion of the profound necessity for faith, hope, and love. If indeed in this difficult and responsible phase of the history of the Church and of humankind, we feel a special need to have recourse to Christ, Who is Lord of His Church and Lord of human history in virtue of the mystery of the Redemption, we believe that no one else but Mary will know how to introduce us into the Divine and human dimension of the mystery.

No one else but Mary has been introduced into it by God Himself. Herein lies the exceptional character of the grace of the Divine Motherhood. It is not only the dignity of the Motherhood that is unique and unrepeatable in the history of the human race. Also unique because of its profundity and fullness of aciton is Mary's participation (by reason of the same Motherhood) in the Divine sign of human salvation, through the mystery of the Redemption.

THE CHURCH LOOKS TO MARY WITH HOPE

THE mystery of the Redemption was formed, so to speak, beneath the heart of the Virgin of Nazareth when she uttered her "Yes." From that moment this virginal and at the same time maternal heart, under the special action of the Holy Spirit, always followed the work of her Son and went out toward all those whom Christ embraced and continually embraces in His inexhaustible love. That is why this heart must be also maternally inexhaustible.

The characteristic of this maternal love, which the Mother of God injects into the mystery of the Redemption and into the life of the Church, is expressed in the fact that it is singularly close to human beings and to all their life circumstances. It is in this that the Mystery of the Mother consists.

The Church, which looks to Mary with love and a most particular hope, desires to appreciate this mystery in an even more profound manner. In this, the Church recognizes the path of her daily life, which every person constitutes.

MOTHER OF CONSOLATION

THE Paschal period in a certain way renders even more evident and meaningful the title of "Consoled" and "Consoler" attributed to Mary most holy. The Church sings at this time: "Queen of

Heaven, rejoice and be glad, alleluia!" In a certain manner she invites Mary to a very special participation in the joy of Christ's Resurrection.

Indeed, Mary who was immersed in the most profound sorrow during the Passion, Agony, and Death on the Cross of her Divine Son Jesus, has been "consoled" much more than all others by His glorious Resurrection.

Her sorrow was immense and unspeakable. But then her consolation was also immense!

MARY STRENGTHENS OUR FAITH

THE fullness of joy and consolation runs throughout the whole Paschal Mystery because of the fact that the Crucified Christ died for us, that He rose, and that He conquered death as He had predicted. Such fullness is especially found with much superabundance in the heart of Mary. Indeed, it is so superabundant as to become the source of consolation for all who have recourse to her.

This is a question of consolation in the most profound sense of the word. It restores strength to the human spirit, illumines, consoles, and reenforces faith and transforms it into faithful abandonment to Providence and spiritual joy.

LOVING CONSOLATRIX

EVEN the Church, which is a mother after the example of Mary (cf. LG 60-65) strives to impart interior consolation in the Paschal Mystery. This consolation is a true reenforcement of the soul based on the certainty that the Risen Christ is the decisive victory of good, of the salvific reality of God; it is the light, truth, and life for all human beings and forever.

Mary most holy continues to be the loving consolatrix in the countless physical and moral sufferings that afflict and torment humankind. She knows our sufferings and our pains because she too has suffered, from Bethlehem to Calvary: "And a sword shall pierce your own soul" (Lk 2:35).

Mary is our spiritual Mother, and a mother always understands her children and consoles them in their afflictions.

THE MISSION OF THE VIRGIN IN THE PLAN OF SALVATION

THERE is no announcement more joyous and more important for our salvation than the one proclaimed by the Apostles: "The Lord is truly risen!" (Lk 24:34). In Jesus the terrible duel waged between death and life was resolved in favor of life. He is the Living One, the Conqueror of the forces of evil, and the Lord of history (cf. 2 Cor 13:4; Rv 5:5; 1:8).

He has not returned to His former life—which is still doomed to death—like Lazarus, but He has taken on a new and unending life: "Christ, raised from the dead, will never die again; death has no more power over Him" (Rom 6:9).

In His wake Jesus draws all the faithful, for He is "the firstfruits" and "the firstborn from the dead" (1 Cor 15:20; Col 1:18). And, in the first place, He draws His Mother, glorified in consequence of the Risen One, as the Church has always perceived, in harmony with the mission of the Virgin Mary in the plan of salvation.

SHE LIVES WITH THE LORD

THAT is why we too, in union with the Christian generations that have gone before us, have the joy of proclaiming the happy announcement: "Mary lives with the Lord; she lives a full and unending life! Even on her, thanks to God's grace, death has no more effect!"

This conviction lies behind the confident prayer that at least from the third century the faithful have been addressing to Mary, invoking her in the anthem "Sub tuum praesidium" (Under your protection) as the holy Mother of God, endowed with power, purity, and mercy. With immense joy we contemplate Mary living and glorified in the wake of the Risen One. In her we see prefigured the destiny of the Church.

If we are faithful to Christ, we too will meet with Mary's fate and see the doors of life flung open for us. May her example confirm our certainty, and may her prayer sustain our journey and our hope.

EXTRAORDINARY GUIDE

D URING the Easter Season we have examined more deeply, in the Liturgy, the various aspects of the Redemption, which is the announcement of life, hope, and liberation. We have reflected on the Merciful Love of God, Who offers to all the possibility of being freed from evil and from its root, which is sin.

We should, therefore, have confidence in God's Merciful Love and at the same time sincerely acknowledge our condition as lowly and sinful creatures. This is the first step in order to obtain liberation from all evil. This liberation is obtained only by encountering the Crucified and Risen Christ.

In this path to liberation from evil and sin and in this encounter with Christ, we have an extraordinary guide and a powerful believer in the person who was associated in a unique way in the Work of the Redemption: Mary most holy, Mother of the Redeemer and our Mother.

MOTHER OF CHRIST THE LIBERATOR

T HE Blessed Virgin is invoked by the Church under various titles, among which an essentially significant one is that of "Liberatrix," which the Popes have used for centuries in having recourse to her.

People who have recourse to Mary with this hope are those afflicted by evil. They ask her for help.

consolation, and hope. Through her they offer to God the sorrows, sufferings, and crosses that never fail to be part of everyone's life. They ask her, our Liberatrix, to intercede with Him Who alone can take away evil and sin.

Yes, know that Mary most holy, Mother of the Redeemer and our Mother, wishes to lead you to the encounter with Christ the Liberator. Guided by her motherly hand, day after day, you are called to ever renewed encounters with the Christ Who delivers us from evil.

STRENGTHEN YOUR DROOPING HANDS!

AS the Letter to the Hebrews declares, "Strengthen your drooping hands and your tottering knees. Walk along straight paths, so that your halting limbs may not be dislocated but healed" (Heb 12:12).

While you implore the health of body and soul, know how to offer, through Mary most holy, your sufferings to Christ, so that you too may become, like her, instruments of liberation from every form of evil that oppresses people and the world.

May the Blessed Virgin ever be your light, your hope, and direct your thoughts to that Homeland in which there is neither evil nor death.

THE BLESSEDNESS OF FAITH

"BLESSED is she who has believed that the Lord's words to her would be fulfilled" (Lk 1:45).

With this greeting the aged Elizabeth exalts her young cousin Mary, who has come in humility and purity to offer her services.

Under the impulsion of the Holy Spirit, the Mother of the Baptist is the first in the history of the Church to proclaim the greatness of God's work accomplished in the Virgin of Nazareth, and she sees "the blessedness of faith" fully realized in Mary, because she has believed that the Lord's words to her would be fulfilled.

We should reflect on what constituted the basic inner attitude of the Blessed Virgin toward God: her faith!

"ANYONE WHO DOES NOT TAKE UP THE CROSS . . . "

MARY has believed! She has trusted the words of the Lord, which were transmitted through the Angel Gabriel. Her most pure heart, already completely given to God from her infancy until the Annunciation, has opened out in a generous and unconditional "Yes" with which she has consented to become the Mother of the Messiah and Son of God.

From that moment on she would insert herself even more deeply in God's plan and let herself be led by the hand of God's mysterious Providence. For her whole life, rooted in faith, she would spiritually follow her Son. She would become the first and perfect "disciple" and realize daily the demands of such a following in accord with the words of Jesus: "Anyone who does not take up the cross and follow Me cannot be My disciple" (Lk 14:27).

"ALL AGES TO COME SHALL CALL ME BLESSED"

MARY will go forward throughout her life in the "pilgrimage of faith" (cf. LG 58) while her most beloved Son, misunderstood, calumniated, condemned, and crucified, will trace for her day after day a sorrowful way, the necessary prelude to that glorification described by the "Magnificat": "all ages to come shall call me blessed" (Lk 1:48).

But first Mary must herself ascend Calvary to assist in sorrow at the Death of her Son Jesus.

DISINTERESTED LOVE

THE Visitation presents us with another aspect of Mary's interior life: her attitude of "humble service" and "disinterested love" toward whoever is in need.

As soon as she learned from the Angel about the condition of her cousin Elizabeth, she set out without delay for the hill country in order to arrive "in haste" at a town of Judah that is today known as "Ain Karim."

The meeting between the two mothers is also the meeting between the Precursor and the Messiah.

Through the mediation of His Mother the Messiah begins His work of salvation by causing John the Baptist to leap for joy even in his mother's womb.

"WHOEVER LOVES GOD . . ."

"NO one has ever seen God. Yet if we love one another God dwells in us. . . . The command we have from Him is this: whoever loves God must also love his brother" (1 Jn 4:12, 21), St. John the Evangelist would later state.

But who better than Mary put this word into practice? And who else but Jesus, Whom she bore in her womb, moved her, spurred her, and inspired her to this continual attitude of generous service and love toward others?

"The Son of Man . . . has come not to be served by others, but to serve" (Mt 20:28), Jesus will declare to His disciples. But His Mother had already perfectly put into practice this attitude of her Son.

EAGER IN HER JOY

LET us listen once more to the celebrated comment, filled with spiritual unction, that St. Ambrose makes about Mary's journey: "Joyful at fulfilling her desire, delicate in her duty, and eager in her joy, she hastens into the hill country. Where else but toward the heights can she go since she is already filled with God? The grace of the Holy Spirit knows no obstacles that can retard her steps."

And if we reflect with special attention on the Letter to the Romans, we perceive that it provides an effective image of the behavior of Mary most holy for our edification. Her charity was not feigned, and she deeply loved others. She served the Lord with a fervent spirit. She was joyful in hope, patient in tribulation, persevering in prayer, and solicitous for the needs of others (cf. Rom 12:9ff).

JOYFUL IN HOPE

"JOYFUL in hope." The atmosphere that pervades the Gospel episode of the Visitation is one of "joy." The mystery of the Visitation is a "mystery of joy." John the Baptist exults with joy in the womb of his mother. Elizabeth, filled with joy over her gift of motherhood, breaks forth into blessings for the Lord. Mary intones the "Magnificat," a hymn overflowing with Messianic joy.

But what is the mysterious, hidden source of this joy? It is Jesus, Whom Mary has already conceived through the power of the Holy Spirit, and Who already begins to destroy the root cause of fear, anguish, and sadness: sin, the most humiliating slavery for human beings.

YOUR FRUIT IS BLESSED

"BLESSED is she who has believed" (Lk 1:45). These words were addressed to Mary of Nazareth by her cousin Elizabeth during the visitation.

They form part of the "second salutation" that Mary has received. "The first" was that of the Angel at the moment of the Annunciation: "Hail, full of grace. The Lord is with you" (Lk 1:28). This is the expression used by Gabriel, the messenger sent by God to Nazareth in Galilee.

On the occasion of Mary's visit to the house of Zechariah, "this salutation of the Angel" finds its human complement on the lips of Elizabeth: "Blessed are you among women and blessed is the fruit of your womb" (Lk 1:42).

THE MOTHER OF THE LORD COMES

ELIZABETH'S human salutation and that of the Angel to Mary are impregnated with the same light.

Both form a unified whole. Both have become part of our prayer to the Mother of God, "the prayer of the Church." "Who am I that the Mother of my Lord should come to me?" (Lk 1:43).

Elizabeth was the first to "profess the faith of the Church": Mother of my Lord, Mother of God, Theotokos!

"Blessed is she who has believed that the Lord's words to her would be fulfilled" (Lk 1:45).

Today, these words of Elizabeth addressed to Mary at the Visitation are repeated by the whole Church.

SHE BELIEVED IN THIS MYSTERY

WITH Elizabeth's words to Mary, the whole Church blesses above all God Himself: "Blessed be the God and Father of our Lord Jesus Christ" (1 Pt 1:3).

Our Lord Jesus Christ is the Son. He is of the same nature as God. He became man by the power of the Holy Spirit. He took flesh at the Annunciation in the womb of the Virgin of Nazareth, and He was born of her as a true man. He is God made Man.

Concretely, this took place in Mary at the moment of the Annunciation by the Angel. And in this mystery, she was the first to believe. She trusted God Himself on the words of the Angel.

She said "Yes," let it be done to me as you say. "Behold, I am the servant of the Lord."

THE FAITH OF MARY

WITH the words of Peter the Apostle, the Church unites herself to Mary in her faith.

"Blessed be the God and Father of our Lord Jesus Christ! In His great mercy He has given us a new birth through the Resurrection of Jesus Christ from the dead, a birth into a living hope and into an imperishable inheritance, incapable of fading or defilement. This inheritance is kept in heaven for you who through faith are guarded by the power of God until the coming of the salvation that will be revealed in the last days" (1 Pt 1:3-5).

This is the faith of the Church and the hope of the Church. But above all else this is the faith of Mary. She has a part, a supereminent one, in the Church's faith and hope. She believed before the Apostles.

When His relatives did not believe in Jesus (cf. Jn 7:5) and the crowds had more enthusiasm than faith, Mary already had an unshakable faith.

MODEL OF THE CHURCH

MARY is the "primordial Model of the Church" who walks along the path of faith and along the path of hope. Along the path of faith, hope, and charity.

In the Constitution on the Church, the Second Vatican Council expressed itself this way: "The Mother of God is a type of the Church in the order of faith, charity, and perfect union with Christ. . . . By her belief and obedience . . . as the new Eve she brought forth on earth the very Son of the Father, showing an undefiled faith, not in the word of the ancient serpent, but in that of God's messenger. The Son Whom she brought forth is He Whom God placed as the firstborn among many brothers and sisters (cf. Rom 8:29), namely the faithful, in whose birth and education she cooperates with a maternal love" (LG 63).

THE FAITH OF THE MOTHER OF GOD

THE words addressed by God to Mary have been fulfilled. This "fulfillment" is called Jesus Christ.

When the Risen One appeared to the Apostles after His Passion, one of them, Thomas, who was absent at that moment, refused to believe.

One week later Thomas saw Christ and proclaimed: "My Lord and my God!" (Jn 20:28). And he heard the Master tell him: "Because you have seen Me, you have believed. Blessed are they who will believe without seeing" (Jn 20:29).

And you, dear brothers and sisters, "although you have never seen Christ, you love Him; and although you do not see Him now, you believe in Him" (1 Pt 1:8).

In this faith you find an aid in Mary, the Mother of Christ: she was the first to believe! She will lead you to Him!

Let us pray for our generation, that future generations will participate in the faith of the Mother of God.

This faith helps you to bear the pain and sufferings of life; it helps you "to persevere in hope" even through "many trials." Above all, these "trials will verify the genuine quality of your faith, which is far more precious than gold, which is tried by fire even though it is destined to perish" (1 Pt 1:7).

THE HUMBLE SERVANT

L ET us pray that our generation may have a faith that is knowing and rich in maturity, a faith ready for any trial! May such a faith be a participation in the faith of Mary, who stands upright at the foot of her Son's Cross on Calvary.

Was not Mary's great trial to see her Son rejected and condemned to death by the leaders of His people? Yet she followed Him till the very end.

She shared in everything. She united herself with Jesus Who offered His life for the salvation of the world.

As for us, when God seems far away, when we do not understand His ways, when the cross hurts our shoulders and our heart, when we suffer on account of our faith, let us learn from Mary how to have faith, let us learn from our Mother how to have faith in trials and how to obtain strength and courage from an unconditional adherence to Jesus Christ.

This is how Mary was able to repeat in a singular manner these words, uttered in her "Magnificat": "He has looked upon His servant in her lowliness" (Lk 1:48).

THE MYSTERY OF FAITH

M ARY'S "humility" is associated in a salvific union with her Crucified Son's "divestiture!"

The whole Church, gazing on Mary at the foot of the Cross, repeats with special exultation: "Blest is she who has believed. . . ."

And behold, this faith of Mary at the foot of the Cross appears like "the first dawn of Easter morn."

The Cross and the Resurrection unite in a single mystery: the Paschal Mystery.

The Church lives this mystery from day to day.

She meditates on it in prayer, and here the prayer of the Rosary takes on all its importance. It is with Mary, in the rhythm of the Angelic salutation, that we enter into the whole mystery of her Son, made flesh, put to death, and risen for us. In the life of every Christian, of every family, this Marian prayer must constitute, as it were, daily respiration.

The Church meditates on but also celebrates the ineffable Paschal Mystery every day in the Eucharist. With Mary we approach the source, we unite with the offering of her Son, and we are nourished by His life: "the Mystery of Faith."

THE SECRET OF JOY

D AY after day, the Church expresses her exuberant joy before this "Mystery of Faith," extracting its secret from the heart of the Mother of Christ at the moment when she chants the "Magnificat": "My soul proclaims the greatness of the Lord. . . . God Who is mighty has done great things for me, and holy is His Name" (Lk 1:46, 49).

We learn from Mary 'the secret of joy," which comes from faith, to illumine our lives and the lives of others.

The Gospel of the Visitation is replete with joy: the joy of being visited by God, the joy of opening the doors to the Redeemer. This joy is the fruit of the Holy Spirit, and no one can take it away from us if we remain faithful to Him.

ONE HEART AND ONE MIND

O MOTHER,
Mother of God and Mother of the Church,
in this house so significant for us,
we are one heart and one mind:
like Peter, the Apostles, and the brothers
united in prayer,
with you in the Upper Room (cf. Acts 1:14).

We entrust our lives to you,
for you welcomed with absolute fidelity
the word of God
and dedicated yourself
to His plan of salvation and grace,
adhering with total docility
to the action of the Holy Spirit.

You also received from your Son
the mission to welcome and take care of
the disciple whom He loved (cf. Jn 20:26).

Each and every one of us say to you,
"Totus tuus sum ego,"
"I am all yours,"

so that you may take our consecration
and unite it with that of Jesus and with yours,
as an offering to the Father
for the life of the world.

MARY RECALLS THE SALVIFIC VALUE OF THE WORK OF CHRIST

AFTER the Ascension of Jesus, the first disciples were gathered together with "Mary the Mother of Jesus" (Acts 1:14).

In their community, therefore, there was also Mary; in fact, it was probably she who gave them their cohesiveness.

And the fact that she is described as "the Mother of Jesus" indicates how greatly she was related to the person of her Son. It indicates that Mary recalls only and always the salvific work of Jesus, our unique Savior. It also indicates that belief in Jesus cannot dispense us from also including in our act of faith the figure of the woman who was His Mother.

THERE IS YOUR MOTHER

IN the family of God, Mary protects the diversity of each person within the communion of all.

And at the same time she can teach us to be open to the Holy Spirit, to take part in Christ's total submission to His Father's will, and above all to participate intimately in the Passion of the Son and to assure the fruitfulness of our ministry.

"There is your Mother" (Jn 19:7). Each of us must hear these words as addressed to us and take confidence and inspiration from them to advance in an ever more decisive and serene manner along the path of our life.

MARY BEARS WITNESS TO THE POWER OF THE SPIRIT

MARY is the most sublime witness of what the power of the Spirit of God can do in human beings when He renews them interiorly and makes them living stones of a new world. The recipient of the anticipated Grace of the Redeemer, she responded with faithful obedience to every request of God, to every motion of the Holy Spirit.

As a humble servant, she gave herself virginally to the Lord. As a caring sister, she was attentive to the needs of others. As a Mother, she consecrated herself completely to the person and mission of her Redeemer Son, becoming His perfect disciple and generously associating herself with Him in the unique sacrifice that takes away sin and reconciles us with the Father.

The Holy Spirit illumined the obscure path of faith step by step for her, enabled her to grasp every word and every action of her Son, and strengthened her in the sorrow of Calvary and the supreme offering. Then, after the Cross, He configured her to her Son in glory.

PRAYERFUL PRESENCE IN THE CHURCH

PENTECOST speaks to us of Mary's presence in the Church: her prayerful presence in the Church of the Apostles and in the Church of all ages. In her place as a simple faithful but as the first among the faithful, insofar as she is Mother she sustains the common prayer and unites her voice to the voice of the Apostles and the other disciples to implore the gift of the Holy Spirit, Who had overshadowed her at the Annunciation, making her the Mother of God.

Annunciation and Pentecost: These are the two moments that mysteriously perpetuate themselves in the Church. What took place at Nazareth and what took place in the Upper Room are realized every day on all the altars of the world. It is in this way that "the Spirit of the Lord fills the universe."

MOTHER OF LOVE AND UNITY

THE experience of the Upper Room would not reflect the time of grace in the effusion of the Spirit if it did not have the joy and presence of Mary. "With Mary, the Mother of Jesus" (Acts 1:14), we read concerning the great moment of Pentecost. And it is this moment that we wish to experience and renew.

That is why, with the Church's very rich Marian tradition, we unite ourselves to the Blessed Virgin. May she who is the Mother of love and unity bind us profoundly together so that like the first Christian community born in the Upper Room we may be "one single heart and one single soul."

Mary is the "Mother of unity," and in her womb the Son of God united Himself to all humankind, mystically inaugurating the Lord's marriage union with all human beings. May she now help us to be "one" and to become instruments of unity among our faithful and among all other human beings.

PRAYER FOR ALL PRIESTS

O MOTHER of the Church,
I address a special supplication to you
for all priests who work on the earth,
so that they may become "servants of Christ
and administrators of the mysteries of God"
   (1 Cor 4:1).
for the good of their brothers and sisters.

Assist them with your protection.

Help also religious men,
religious women, and catechists,
so that by their dedication and witness
they may help their brothers and sisters
to faithfully follow Christ,
"the Way, the Truth, and the Life."

May their example be the seed
of many holy vocations.

May the Word of God,
Who became Man in your virginal womb
through the power of the Holy Spirit,
grow in our hearts
and radiate forth more extensively
for the salvation of the whole world!

BORN OF THE VIRGIN MARY

AVE verum Corpus natum/ex Maria Virgine . . ." (Hail, O True Body, born/of the Virgin Mary . . .).

While we wish to manifest a special devotion toward the Eucharist, toward the Most Holy Body of Jesus, our thoughts turn to her from whom God, the Son of God, has taken this Body: the Virgin whose name is Mary.

MARY PREPARED
HIS BODY AND HIS BLOOD

ON the feast of the Most Holy Body of Christ, our "thanks" rises in acknowledgment to the Father, Who has given us the Divine Word, the living Bread come down from heaven, and rises with joy to the Virgin, who offered to the Lord the innocent Flesh and precious Blood that we receive on the altar.

"Ave, verum Corpus" (Hail, true Body): True Body, totally conceived by the power of the Holy

Spirit, borne in the womb with ineffable love, born for us from the Virgin Mary: "natum de Maria Virgine."

This Body with this Blood—which after the Consecration is present on the altar, and is offered to the Father, and becomes a communion of love for all, strengthening us in the unity of the Spirit to found the Church—preserves its original Marian matrix

It is Mary who prepared that Flesh and that Blood before offering both to the Word as a gift from the whole human family, so that He might unite with them in becoming our Redeemer, the High Priest and Victim.

AT THE ROOT OF THE EUCHARIST

A T the root of the Eucharist there is the virginal and maternal life of Mary, her overflowing experience of God, her way of faith and love, which through the power of the Holy Spirit made a temple out of her flesh and an altar out of her heart. For she conceived not through nature but through faith, by a free and conscious act—an act of obedience.

And if the Body that we eat and the Blood that we drink is the inestimable gift of the Risen Lord to us, on our pilgrim way, it also carries with it, like sweet-smelling bread, the taste and fragrance of the Virgin Mary.

"Vere passum, immolatum in cruce pro homine."
That Body has truly suffered and has been immolated on the Cross for human beings.

SHE CONSENTED
TO THE IMMOLATION OF HER SON

BORN of the Virgin Mary to be the pure, holy, and immaculate oblation, Christ accomplished on the altar of the Cross the unique and perfect sacrifice, which every Mass in an unbloody way renews and renders present.

In this unique sacrifice Mary, the first among the redeemed and the Mother of the Church, had an active part. She stood beneath the Cross, suffering profoundly in union with her only-begotten Son. She associated herself with a maternal spirit in His sacrifice. She consented with love to His immolation (LG 58). She offered Him and she offered herself to the Father.

Every Eucharist is the memorial of this Sacrifice and this Pasch that restored life to the world. Every Mass puts us in intimate communion with Christ's Mother, whose sacrifice "becomes present" as the sacrifice of her Son "becomes present" at the words of the Consecration of bread and wine pronounced by the priest.

THE HOUSE OF MARY

THE figure of St. Ann recalls the paternal house of Mary, the Mother of Christ.

It is there that Mary came into the world, bearing in herself that extraordinary mystery of the Immaculate Conception.

It is there that Mary was surrounded by the love and care of her parents: Joachim and Ann.

It is there that Mary "learned" from her mother St. Ann how to be a mother.

And although from the human standpoint she had renounced motherhood, the Heavenly Father, accepting her total self-giving, enriched her with the most perfect and most holy Motherhood.

From the height of the Cross, Christ in a certain sense extended the Motherhood of His Mother to His beloved disciple and similarly extended it to the whole Church and all human beings.

GOD HAS GIVEN GRACE

WHEN as "heirs of the Divine promise" (cf. Gal 4:28, 31) we find ourselves within the radius of Mary's Motherhood, and when we experience anew her holy profundity and fullness, we then reflect that it was proper for St. Ann to be the first to teach Mary, her daughter, how to be a Mother.

"Ann" in Hebrew signifies "God [subject understood] has given grace." When he reflected on this meaning of St. Ann's name, St. John Damascene exclaimed:

"Since it was to come to pass that the Virgin Mother of God should be born of Ann, nature did not dare to precede the seed of grace. It remained without its proper fruit so that grace might produce its own. For that firstborn daughter was to be born who would in turn give birth to the firstborn of all creation."

MARY IS CLOSE TO THE HOLY TRINITY

JESUS has revealed to us the secrets of the Divine life and its manifestation in the world, announcing that the one God is in three equal and distint Persons: the Father, creator of heaven and earth; the Son, Who became Man for the salvation of the human race; and the Holy Spirit, Who proceeds from the Father and the Son to build up the Church and accomplish every work of sanctification.

In the present prayer meeting we wish to unite the adoration of this Mystery with the veneration of that creature to whom more than any other it has been given to understand this Trinity and to have—we might say—an "intimate experience" of it: Mary, the Mother of God.

For Mary's communion with the Three Divine Persons is most special and unique. Made fecund by the Holy Spirit, she is the Mother of the Incarnate Word, and her Son is thus the very Son of the Father. Who then more than she is close to the Blessed Trinity? What creature more than Mary can help us to know and love the Trinity?

ORDINARY TIME

MADE ONE WITH THE UNITY OF FATHER, SON, AND HOLY SPIRIT

THE Church, as the Second Vatican Council affirms is "a people made one with the unity of the Father, the Son, and the Holy Spirit" (LG 4), and Mary is the Mother of the Church. This indicates that it is solely through Mary's motherly intercession that we can ever better comprehend how the Holy Spirit constitutes, preserves, and perfects the unity of the Church, leading her in history to the fullness of truth.

The Blessed Virgin is the chosen dwelling of the Most Holy Trinity, the temple where the glory of the Trinity dwells (cf. Ps 26: 8). It is she who obtains from her Son the grace for us also to be temples of God, inhabited and moved by the Spirit of the Lord (cf. 1 Cor 3:16). It is thanks to Mary's prayer that the Church grows "as a holy temple in the Lord" (Eph 2:21).

THE DAWN OF A BETTER WORLD

"I WANT to recite with you the Angelus": the prayer of Nazareth, the prayer of the Annunciation.

We recite it "on the day of the Assumption of Mary into heaven."

The Annunciation resounds in this prayer like a final accord. This is "an accord of glorification," which is joined to all the mysteries of the earthly life of the Mother of God: joyful and sorrowful.

The Assumption itself of the Mother in heaven completes the glorious mysteries of her Son: the Resurrection and Ascension into heaven.

In the footsteps of the One Who has risen and ascended to heaven, Mary His Mother is assumed into heaven and "crowned" with the glory that befits the Mother of God.

I also want to turn my gaze toward her whom Paul VI called in prophetic fashion "the Dawn of a better world."

No matter how much the world may weigh upon us, no matter how much evil, sin, and suffering it may hold, the gaze of faith, fixed on the Mother of God, always discovers in her the "Dawn of a better world."

This is the special fruit of the feast of Mary's Assumption into heaven.

"MY SOUL PROCLAIMS THE GREATNESS OF THE LORD"

WE are on the "threshold of the house of Zechariah," in the locality of Ain Karim. Mary arrives here, bearing in her the joyful mystery—the mystery of a God Who has become Man in her womb. Mary meets Elizabeth, a person who is very close to her and with whom she is united by an analogous mystery. Mary comes to share her joy with Elizabeth.

On the threshold of the house of Zechariah a blessing awaits Mary, a blessing that is the sequel to what she has heard from the lips of Gabriel: "Blessed are you among women and blessed is the fruit of your womb. . . . Blessed is she who has believed that the Lord's words to her would be fulfilled" (Lk 1:42, 45).

And at that moment from Mary's innermost being, from the depths of her silence, flows forth the chant that expresses the whole truth of the great Mystery. It is the canticle that announces the History of Salvation and lays bare the heart of Mary: "My soul proclaims the greatness of the Lord . . ." (Lk 1:46).

ON THE THRESHOLD OF ETERNITY

TODAY we are no longer on the threshold of the house of Zechariah at Ain Karim. We are on the threshold of eternity. The life of the Mother of Christ has come to an end on earth.

In her is now to be accomplished the law that Paul the Apostle proclaimed in his First Letter to the Corinthians: the law of death overcome by Christ's Resurrection.

In reality, "Christ has risen from the dead, the firstfruits of those who have fallen asleep. . . . Just as in Adam all die, so in Christ all will come to life again, but each in proper order" (1 Cor 15:20-23)

In this order, Mary is the first. Who, indeed, more than she "belongs to Christ"?

Therefore, at the moment when the law of death overcome by the Resurrection of her Son is accomplished in Mary, she gives forth from her heart the canticle that is a canticle of salvation and grace: "the canticle of her Assumption into heaven."

"MY SPIRIT REJOICES"

THIS new truth echoes forth in these new words, which Mary uttered one day during her visit to Elizabeth: "My spirit rejoices in God my Savior. . . . God Who is mighty has done great things for me" (Lk 1:47f).

God has done them from the beginning:

—from the moment of her conception in the womb of her mother Ann, when after choosing her to be the Mother of His own Son, He freed her from the yoke of the inheritance of original sin;

—then during the years of her childhood when He called her totally to Himself, to His service, like the Spouse in the Song of Songs;

—then through the Annunciation at Nazareth and through the night of Bethlehem and through the thirty years of hidden life in the house of Nazareth.

"HOLY IS HIS NAME"

GOD continued to do great things for Mary, successively, through the experiences of the teaching years of her Son the Christ, the sufferings of the Cross, and the dawn of the Resurrection. Truly, "God Who is mighty has done great things for me, and holy is His Name" (Lk 1:48f).

Mary glorifies God, aware that in virtue of His grace all generations shall glorify her because "His mercy is from age to age on those who fear Him" (Lk 1:50).

MARY'S SPIRITUAL TESTAMENT

WE too praise God in unison for all that He has done for the humble Servant of the Lord. We glorify Him. We give Him thanks.

The words of the "Magnificat" manifest the whole heart of our Mother. Today they constitute "her spiritual testament." Every one of us should look at our life and the history of humankind in a certain sense with the eyes of Mary.

In this respect, St. Ambrose has left us some beautiful words, which I wish to repeat for you today: "May the soul of Mary be in each one of us to proclaim the greatness of the Lord, and may the spirit of Mary be in each one of us to rejoice in God. Only one is the Mother of God according to the flesh; but according to faith, all souls engender Christ. Each person, in fact, welcomes the Word of God in his or her heart."

A NEW VISION OF LIFE

SHOULD not we too say with Mary: "God Who is mighty has done great things for me"? For what He did in her He has also done for us and to us.

For us, He became Man, and to us He brought light and truth. He makes us children of God and heirs of heaven.

"Mary's words give us a new vision of life"—a vision of persevering and coherent faith.

A faith that is the light of daily life, the light of those at times tranquil but often stormy and difficult days.

A faith that illumines, finally, the darkness of death in each one of us.

May this attitude on life and death be the fruit of the feast of the Assumption.

MARY PARTICIPATES IN HER SON'S GLORY

MARY participates in her Son's glory, in that glory whose beginning was 'His Resurrection." This is what St. Paul tells us by the inspired words of the First Letter to the Corinthians: "Just as in Adam all die, so in Christ all will come to life. . . . Christ the firstfruits and then . . . all those who belong to Him" (1 Cor 15:22f).

And who more than His Mother belongs to Christ? Therefore, she is the first to participate in the glory of the Resurrection through her Assumption.

ASSUMED INTO HEAVENLY GLORY

IT is the glory of Mary—which the whole Church both in the East and in the West has experienced for generations—that I wish to profess with you, rejoicing over it as the hearts of all believers rejoice.

Let us recall together, for the consolation and strength of our faith, the dogmatic definition pronounced by Pope Pius XII of happy memory on November 1, 1950:

"By the authority of our Lord Jesus Christ, of the Blessed Apostles Peter and Paul, and by our own proper authority we pronounce, declare, and define as Divinely revealed dogma that Mary, Immaculate Mother of God ever Virgin, after finishing the course of her life on earth, was taken up in soul and body to heavenly glory."

THE MYSTERY OF THE ASSUMPTION

"YOUR throne, O God, lasts forever;
    Your royal scepter is one of justice. . . .
The King's Daughter is all glorious,
    her gown woven of spun gold" (Ps 45:7, 14).

The Liturgy of the Church has recourse to the words of the Psalm to present a great mystery of faith in human images.

It is the mystery of the Assumption of the most holy Mother of God, the Virgin Mary.

Nonetheless, "her own words" are even more eloquent than the comparisons drawn from Psalm 45. Here they are: Mary presents herself at the threshold of the house of her cousin Elizabeth and—greeted by Elizabeth as "the Mother of my Lord"—she utters the words of the "Magnificat":

"My soul proclaims the greatness of the Lord, my spirit rejoices in God my Savior. . . . God Who is mighty has done great things for me, and holy is His Name" (Lk 1:46f, 49).

MARY PRAISES THE "MIGHTY" GOD

"GOD Who is mighty has done great things for me."

When Mary uttered these words, the "Mystery of the Incarnation" had already been accomplished in her through the intermediary of the "announcement of the Angel." The Son of God, the Eternal Word, had become Man in her womb by the power of the Holy Spirit.

As she hastened "into the hill country" to visit Elizabeth, Mary was already "the Mother of the Son of God": she bore within herself the greatest mystery in history.

From the depths of this mystery are born the words of the hymn of the "Magnificat." "From the depths of this mystery" Mary praises the Almighty because He "has done great things" for her (Lk 1:48).

And not only for her—for all humankind. For all human beings and for every individual, God has done "great things" by "becoming Man."

A SPECIAL DIGNITY

THE Virgin of Nazareth has been the object of a special elevation, a special dignity. Behold, she has become the Mother of the God-Man.

"On the day of the Assumption," the Liturgy of the Church places on the lips of Mary her own words: "God Who is mighty has done great things for me."

Between the Visitation and the Assumption there is a "continuity." The one who was chosen from eternity as the Mother of the Incarnate Word, the one in whom "God Himself has dwelt" in the person of the Son of God, Mary in a special way begins to "dwell in God": Father, Son, and Holy Spirit.

This is the mystery that we meditate on with veneration: the mystery of the Assumption.

PRESERVED FROM THE LAW OF DEATH

THE One in whom God Himself made His dwelling in the Person of the Son "was conceived immaculate": she is free from the heritage of original sin.

In this way she has also been preserved "from the law of death," which entered the history of humankind together with sin.

St. Paul writes: "Death came through a man; hence the resurrection of the dead comes through a man also. Just as in Adam all die, so in Christ all will come to life again, but each one in proper order" (1 Cor 15:21-23).

FREE FROM ORIGINAL SIN

FREE—by the work of Christ—from original sin, "redeemed in a particular and exceptional manner," Mary is also included in His Resurrection in a particular and exceptional manner. "The Resurrection of Christ has already overcome the law of sin and death in her" through her Immaculate Conception.

Hence, "there has already been accomplished in her the victory over sin and over the law of death, the penalty for sin; and today 'it is revealed in all its fullness.'"

It was necessary that the one who was Mother of the Risen One should be "the first among human beings" to participate in the powerful fullness of His Resurrection.

A GREAT SIGN IN THE SKY

IT was necessary that she in whom the Son of God and author of the victory over sin and death came to dwell should be the first to dwell in God, free from sin and the corruption of the tomb—from sin by the Immaculate Conception and from the corruption of the tomb by the Assumption.

We believe that "Mary, after finishing the course of her life on earth, was taken up in body and soul to heavenly glory" (Pope Pius XII).

Let us contemplate the Mother of God in a particular way.

Let us fix our gaze on her in her definitive dwelling in God in glory.

She is the "great sign" that, according to the words of St. John in the Book of Revelation, has appeared in the sky (cf. Rv 12:1).

THE DEFINITIVE VICTORY

THE sign is at the same time closely "united with the earth." It is first of all "the sign of the struggle 'with the dragon' " (cf. Rv 12:4), and in this struggle we reread the whole history of the Church on earth: the struggle with Satan, the struggle with the "powers of darkness," who do not cease to unleash their attacks against the Kingdom of God.

At the same time, it is "the sign of the definitive victory" about which the author of the Book of Revelation speaks: "Now have salvation and power come, the Kingdom of our God and the authority of His Anointed One" (Rv 12:10).

WE MUST DWELL IN GOD

WE must "sharpen the eyes of faith" so that the mystery of the Assumption can operate freely in our minds and in our hearts: so that it may become "for us too" the sign of the definitive victory, which is preceded by trials and by struggle in the confrontations with the powers of darkness.

We must "sharpen the eyes of faith" so that we may discern through the trials and tribulations of time "the definitive dimension of eternity": like the Mother of Christ we too must dwell "with God," through eternal union with Him.

GOD DWELLS IN US

WE must comport ourselves in such a way while living on earth that God may live "in us!" In Mary, in whom He made His dwelling through the mystery of the Incarnation as Son in the womb of His Mother, He dwelled first of all "by Grace."

And even in us He wants to dwell by Grace: "Hail Mary, full of grace. . . ."

May the Blessed Virgin revive in us the ardent "desire to live in grace," to persevere in the grace of God.

DEFINITIVE UNION WITH GOD

WE pronounce these words "full of grace" while thinking of the Assumption of Mary. The "fullness of Grace" that Mary enjoyed from the first instant of her conception by reason of the merits of Christ "is confirmed by her Assumption in soul and body."

The Assumption signifies definitive union with God: Father, Son, and Holy Spirit. Grace leads to this union and gradually realizes it during our earthly human existence.

In heaven, "it is definitively realized." "Heaven" is the state of the conclusive and irreversible union with God in the mystery of the Holy Trinity.

The grace of God "prepares" human beings for this state: sanctifying grace with all the actual graces and all the gifts of the Holy Spirit.

FULL OF SUPERNATURAL GIFTS

WHEN, on the day of the Assumption, we say "full of grace," we are thinking of "the fullness" of those "supernatural gifts" that have prepared the Mother of God for glorification in the heart of the Blessed Trinity.

At the same time, we also think of the Grace of God that "works in each of us."

We bear within us a gift that surpasses the limits of time and, triumphing over sin and death, prepares each one of us for the union with God in eternity.

THE SIGN OF THE DIVINITY

A "GREAT sign" appeared in the sky: "a woman clothed with the sun" (Rv 12:1). It is the solemnity of Mary's Assumption into heaven: behold, the Sign attains its fullness. A woman is clothed with "the sun of the Inscrutable Divinity." The sun of the Impenetrable Trinity.

"Full of grace": she is filled with the Father and the Son and the Holy Spirit when They give Themselves to her as one God, the God of creation and revelation, the God of the Covenant and the Redemption, the God of the beginning and the end. The Alpha and the Omega. The God-Who-Is-Love and the God-Who-Is-Grace.

A woman clothed with sun. It is the "Sign of the Assumption into heaven," which is accomplished above the earth and at the same time rises up from the earth.

THE THREE ASPECTS OF THE ASSUMPTION

WE might say that the Liturgy shows us Mary's Assumption into heaven under three aspects. "The first aspect" is "the Visitation" in the house of Zechariah. Elizabeth says: "Blessed are you among women and blessed is the fruit of your womb. . . .

Blessed is she who has believed that the Lord's words to her would be fulfilled" (Lk 1:42, 45).

Mary "believed" in the words that were spoken to her on the part of the Lord, and Mary "welcomed" the Word Who took flesh in her and Who is the fruit of her womb.

The "Redemption of the world" was founded on the faith of Mary; it was tied in with her "Yes" at the beginning of the Annunciation. But its accomplishment began with the fact that "the Word was made flesh and dwelt among us" (Jn 1:14).

THE HYMN OF THE ASSUMPTION

AT the time of the Visitation, Mary, on the threshold of the hospitable house of Zechariah and Elizabeth, utters a sentence that concerns the beginning of the mystery of the Redemption. She says: "God Who is mighty has done great things for me, and holy is His Name" (Lk 1:49).

This sentence, taken in the context of the Visitation, is inserted in the Liturgy of the Assumption. The entire "Magnificat" uttered at the time of the Visitation becomes in the Liturgy "the hymn of Mary's Assumption into heaven."

The Virgin of Nazareth spoke these words when, by her work, the Son of God was to be born on earth. With how much greater reason she could speak them again when, by the work of her Son, she herself is to be born in heaven!

THE ASSUMPTION
AND THE VICTORY OVER DEATH

THE Liturgy reveals to us the second aspect of the Assumption with "the words" of St. Paul in the First Letter to the Corinthians.

The Assumption of the Mother of Christ into heaven forms part of the victory over death, that victory whose beginning is found in Christ's Resurrection: "Christ is now raised from the dead, the firstfruits of those who have fallen asleep" (1 Cor 15:20).

Death is the inheritance of human beings in the wake of original sin: "In Adam all die" (1 Cor 15:22).

The Resurrection wrought by Christ has allowed "this inheritance to be overcome": "'In Christ all will come to life again, but each in proper order: Christ the firstfruits and then . . . all those who belong to Him" (1 Cor 15:22f)

And who more than His Mother belongs to Christ?

MARY'S CONSENT

WHO more than Mary has been redeemed by Christ? Who has cooperated in His Redemption more closely than Mary by her "Yes" at the Annunciation and by her "Yes" at the foot of the Cross?

Thus it is at the very heart of the Redemption accomplished by the Cross on Calvary, it is "by the very power of the Redemption" revealed in the Resurrection, that there is found "the source" for the victory over death experienced by the Mother of the Redeemer, that is, her "Assumption into heaven."

Such is the second aspect of the Assumption that the Liturgy reveals to us.

The third aspect is expressed by the words of the Responsorial Psalm, and it is the poetic language of this Psalm that reveals it: the daughter of the king, arrayed in gold, enters to take her "seat beside the throne of the king": "Your throne, O God, lasts forever; Your royal scepter is one of justice" (Ps 45:7).

In the Redemption is renewed the Kingdom of God, which was begun by creation itself then snuffed out of the human heart by sin.

BIRTH IN HEAVEN

MARY, the Mother of the Redeemer, is the first to "share in this Kingdom of glory and union with God" in eternity.

Her birth in heaven is the definitive beginning of the glory that the sons and daughters of this earth are to attain in God Himself by virtue of Christ's Redemption.

Indeed, the Redemption is the foundation "of the transformation of the history of the cosmos into the Kingdom of God."

Mary is the first among the redeemed.

In her, therefore, the transformation of the history of the cosmos into the Kingdom of God has already begun.

It is this that expresses the mystery of her Assumption into heaven: birth in heaven with body and soul.

BE A WITNESS FOR GOD

O MOTHER,
with your Assumption into heaven
you obtained the complete victory
over the death of soul and body.
Save the sons and daughters of this earth
from the death of the soul!
O Mother of the Church,
in the face of a humankind
that daily seems more fascinated
by everything that is earthly
—and in which the "domination over the world"
prevails over the perspective
of the eternal destiny of human beings in God—
be a witness for God!
You are His Mother.
Who can contest
the witness of a mother?
You have been born through the labors of the earth:

"conceived immaculate!
You have been born to the glory of heaven:
"assumed into heaven!"
You have been clothed
with the sun of the inscrutable Divinity,
with the sun of the impenetrable Trinity,
filled with the Father, the Sun and the Holy Spirit!
To you the Trinity
gives itself as the only God,
the God of creation and revelation,
the God of the Covenant and the Redemption!
the God of the beginning and the end.
The Alpha and the Omega.
The God-Who-Is-Love.
The God-Who-Is-Holiness.
The God Who surpasses all things
and embraces all things.
The God Who is "all in all."
You are clothed with the sun!
Our Mother!
Be a witness for God!
Before the world,
before us, poor exiled children of Eve,
be a witness for God!

A WOMAN CLOTHED WITH THE SUN

"A WOMAN clothed with the sun"
(Rv 12:1).

Today the Church looks to her future. Mary in
her Assumption, Woman clothed with the sun, is a

sign of that future. In her Assumption is manifested "the definitive destiny of human beings," created in the image and likeness of God: the definitive destiny of human beings redeemed by the Crucified Christ. In His Resurrection from the dead and in His Ascension into heaven is inaugurated the "call to glory" of the whole People of God.

"Mary" is the first among the redeemed. She is also the first among those "called to glory."

It is precisely this that the Church celebrates today. Mary the "Woman," "embraced" in soul and body "by the mystery of the Living God: by the Father, by the Son, and by the Holy Spirit."

It is in the light of Mary's Assumption that the Church, looking toward the future, meditates on this subject by "starting from her own past."

THE WOMAN WHO BATTLES
THE SPIRIT OF DARKNESS

THE "Woman clothed with the Sun" cited in John's Book of Revelation is at the same time the "Woman" who after the sin of the human race was introduced into the very center of the struggle against the Spirit of Darkness.

The Book of Genesis speaks about this.

We recall the words of Yahweh addressed to the Tempter: "I will put enmity between you and the woman" (Gn 3:15).

And it is confirmed by the Book of Revelation: "The dragon stood before the woman about to give birth, ready to devour her child when it should be born" (Rv 12:4).

The serpent of the Book of Genesis and the dragon of the Book of Revelation are one and the same: the Spirit of Darkness, the "Father of lies," who, rejecting God and everything that is Divine, has become "negation" incarnate.

The history of the human race and the world takes place "under the incessant pressure" of this original "negation" of God, constantly elaborated by Satan, a negation of the Creator on the part of the creature.

DOING GOD'S WILL

FROM the very beginning, from the moment of the temptation of our first parents, and then throughout all the generations of sons and daughters of the earth, the Tempter has schemed to implant his "I will not serve" in the soul of humans.

"Who is this Woman?" It is she who with all her human existence says: "Behold, I am the servant of the Lord" (Lk 1:38).

She speaks in this way because from her conception her being has been fashioned by the grace of the

One Who was foretold by the Prophets as the "Servant of Yahweh," the One Who coming into the world says: "Behold, I come to do Your will, O God" (Heb 10:7).

He is the Eternal Son of the Father.

At the very core of the struggles between the spirit of the negation of God and salvific service, "the Son of God" became "the Son of Man."

A BOY DESTINED TO RULE ALL THE NATIONS

"SHE gave birth to a Son—a Boy destined to rule all the nations with an iron rod" (Rv 12:5).

Hence, in this way the promise of God in the Book of Genesis is fulfilled: "in the midst of the history of the human race is found the Son of the Woman, Who is the minister of salvation for human beings and for the world."

The struggle and the combat unfold between, on the one hand, the eternal Divine plan of Salvation of everything in God": of human beings and of the world; and on the other hand, the will of Satan that seeks to bring it about that "everything," human beings and the world, rejects God.

We are involved in this struggle.

It unfolds "amid the manifold stories in the history" of humankind on earth.

It is invisible in the heart of every person.

The latest Council has recalled it, especially in various places of the Constitution on the Church in the Modern World ("Gaudium et spes").

"LIKE GODS"

THE Church sees in the solemnity of the Assumption "the synthesis of her own history," from the beginnings of human beings on earth.

In the contemporary mentality, the temptation to reject God and all that is Divine manifests itself in a particularly acute form.

The spirit of falsehood seeks to make the people of our age believe that they are "like gods," beyond good and evil ("knowing good and evil," Gn 3:5), "that sin does not exist even while the reality of sin and evil" assails people as never before, giving proof of its existence by threats on a scale never experienced up to this time!

In the face of all this, "the Church looks to the Woman" as to a great Sign, because "she has never given in to this spirit of falsehood."

THE MYSTERY OF CHRIST

IN the Assumption of Mary, "the Divine plan of salvation for human beings and the world" is reconfirmed. It is reconfirmed in heaven, as the Book of Revelation of John bears witness: "Now have salvation and power come, the Kingdom of our God and the authority of His Anointed One" (Rv 12:10).

In the Assumption of Mary, the Church "meditates" once again on "the whole mystery of Christ": from the beginning of history to its end. She looks at the past and the present in the dimensions of this Mystery.

In it "the future is revealed": the definitive dimension of the history of the human race and the world as well as the definitive form of the life of the Church.

THE SIGN OF THE FUTURE

THE Church meditates on the past and on the present "in the light of the future."

"God's temple in heaven opened and in the temple could be seen the Ark of the Covenant. . . . A great sign appeared in the sky" (Rv 11:19—12:1).

What is the significance of this Sign?

What is the significance of the "Woman clothed with the sun, with the moon under her feet and on her head a crown of twelve stars" (Rv 12:1)?

It signifies precisely the "Future of the world and of the human race" in the Living God: in the Father, in the Son, and in the Holy Spirit.

It signifies "the Kingdom of our God and the authority of His Anointed One."

It signifies "salvation," the triumph of the salvation of God over the denial of God!

In the mystery of her Assumption, "Mary" is "the sign of this Future!"

MARY'S BIRTH PROCLAIMS JOY TO THE WORLD

"**Y**OUR birth, O Virgin Mother of God, proclaims joy to the whole world!"

On September 8, nine months after the feast of the Immaculate Conception of the Mother of God's Son, the Church celebrates the memorial of her birth.

The day of the birth of the Mother directs hearts toward her Son: "From you arose the glorious Sun of Justice, Christ our God; He freed us from the age-old curse and filled us with holiness; He destroyed death and gave us eternal life."

And in this way "the great joy of the Church passes from the Son to the Mother." The day of her birth is truly a preannouncement and the beginning of a better world (" origo mundi melioris"), as Pope Paul VI has proclaimed in stupendous fashion.

And therefore the Liturgy confesses and announces that the birth of Mary radiates its life to all the Churches that are on the globe.

THE HOUSE OF MARY

THE cult rendered to the Mother of God is, according to an ancient tradition, connected with the house of Nazareth—the house in which Mary lived after her espousals with Joseph, the house of the Holy Family.

Every house "is above all a sanctuary of the mother." And she creates it in a special way by her motherhood. It is necessary that the children of the human family, coming into the world, have a roof over their head—that they have a house.

The house of Nazareth, as we know, was not, however, the place of birth of the Son of Mary and the Son of God. Probably every one of Christ's predecessors mentioned in the genealogy of today's Gospel according to Matthew came into the world under the roof of a house. "This was not given to Christ."

THE PLACE THAT HOUSED
THE LIFE OF THE MESSIAH

JESUS was born as an exile at Bethlehem in a manger. And He could not return to the house of Nazareth because He was forced to escape from Herod's cruelty by fleeing from Bethlehem into Egypt, and only after the death of the King did

Joseph dare to bring Mary and the Child into his house at Nazareth.

From then on that house was the place of Jesus' daily life, "the place of the Messiah's hidden life," the house of the Holy Family. It was the first temple, the first church, over which the Mother shone her light as well as her Motherhood.

She bathed it with her light emanating from the great mystery of the Incarnation, from the mystery of her Son.

THE GUARANTEE OF SALVATION

WE celebrate "with joyful hearts the birth of the Virgin Mary, of whom was born the Sun of Justice, Christ our Lord."

This Marian feast constitutes one whole invitation to joy, specifically because by the birth of Mary most holy God gave to the world a kind of concrete guarantee that salvation was now imminent.

Humankind had for thousands of years, in a more or less conscious manner, been waiting for something or someone to set it free from sorrow, from evil, from anguish, and from despair. In the Chosen People, especially the Prophets, it had found the herald of God's reassuring and comforting words.

Now overcome and fearful though it was, it could finally look to this child Mary. She was the point of convergence and point of arrival of a complex Divine promise that found a mysterious echo in the very heart of history.

THE WOMAN OF THE FIRST ANNOUNCEMENT OF REDEMPTION

THE "child" Mary, still petite and fragile, is the "Woman" of the first announcement of the future Redemption, raised up by God in opposition to the tempter serpent: "I will put enmity between you and the Woman, and between your offspring and hers; He will crush your head, while you strike at His heel" (Gn 3:15).

This child is the "Virgin," who is to "be with Child, and bear a Son, Who will be called Emmanuel," which signifies God-is-with-us (cf. Is 7:14).

This child is the "Mother," who is to give birth in Bethlehem to the "One Who is to be ruler in Israel" (cf. Mi 5:1f).

ASSOCIATED WITH THE LIFE OF HER SON

THE Liturgy applies to Mary being born the passage from the Letter to the Romans in which St. Paul describes God's merciful plan for the elect: Mary is predestined by the Trinity for a very sublime mission; she is called; she is sanctified; she is glorified.

God has predestined her to be intimately associated with the life and work of her only Son.

Therefore, He has sanctified her in an admirable and singular fashion, from the first moment of her conception, making her "full of grace" (cf. Lk 1:28). He has conformed her to the image of her Son: such a conformation, we might say, was unique because Mary was the first and most perfect disciple of her Son.

THE DOOR OF GOD

GOD'S plan in Mary has culminated in the glorification that has rendered her mortal body conformed to the glorious Body of the Risen Jesus. The Assumption of Mary body and soul into heaven represents, as it were, the ultimate stage of the vicissitudes of this creature, in whom the Heavenly Father has manifested in an excellent manner His Divine pleasure.

Hence, the whole Church cannot fail to rejoice in this celebration of the Birth of Mary most holy. It is she who—as St. John Chrysostom declares with moving eloquence—is "the virginal and Divine door, from whom and through whom God, Who is above all things, is about to make His entrance corporally on earth."

A FLOWER WILL GROW
FROM THE TRUNK OF JESSE

[ST. John Chrysostom continues:] "Today a shoot will spring up from the trunk of Jesse, and from it a flower substantially united with the Divinity will be born. Today on earth He Who once separated the firmament from the waters and raised it on high has created a heaven for earthly nature, and this heaven is Divinely much more splendid than the first!"

To look to Mary signifies to view ourselves in a model whom God personally has given us for our salvation and our sanctification.

And today Mary teaches us above all to preserve intact "our faith in God," that faith which has been given us at Baptism and which must continually grow and mature in us during the various stages of our Christian lives.

MARY MEDITATED IN HER HEART ON "THE THINGS OF FAITH"

COMMENTING on St. Luke's words: "Mary treasured all these things and meditated on them in her heart" (Lk 2:19), St. Ambrose expresses himself this way: "Let us acknowledge in all things the modesty of the holy Virgin who, without stain in body or in words, meditated in her heart on the things of faith."

We too must continually meditate in our hearts on "the things of faith," that is, we must be open and receptive to the Word of God, so that our daily life—on the personal, familial, and professional level—may be ever in perfect accord and harmonious coherence with the message of Jesus, with the teaching of the Church, and with the examples of the Saints.

"LIKE THE ANGELS OF GOD"

MARY, the Virgin-Mother, reaffirms for us all the very great value of "motherhood," glory and joy of women, and especially the very great value of "Christian virginity" that is professed and embraced "in view of the Kingdom of God" (cf. Mt 19:12), namely, as a testimony, in this fallen world, of that final world in which the saved will be "like the Angels of God" (cf. Mt 22:30).

MOTHER OF CHRISTIAN FAMILIES

WITH complete respect for the freedom of the children of God, the Church has proposed and continues to propose to the faithful a few practices of piety with a special insistence.

Among these is to be mentioned the recitation of the Rosary: "We desire, as a continuation of the thought of our predecessors, to recommend strongly the recitation of the family Rosary. . . . There is no doubt that . . . the Rosary should be considered one of the best and most efficacious prayers in common that the Christian family is invited to recite. We like to think, and sincerely hope, that when the family gathering becomes a time of prayer the Rosary is a frequent and favored manner of praying" (MC 52, 54).

Thus, authentic Marian devotion, which is expressed in the sincere bond with the Blessed Virgin and the imitation of her spiritual attitudes, constitutes a privileged instrument for nourishing the communal love in the family and for developing conjugal and family spirituality. The Mother of Christ and of the Church is thus, in a special way, the Mother of Christian families, which are domestic churches.

A WONDERFUL PRAYER

TODAY I want to draw your attention to the Rosary.

The Rosary is my favorite prayer. It is a wonderful prayer! Wonderful in its simplicity and in its profundity.

In this prayer we repeat many times the words that the Virgin Mary heard from the Archangel and from her cousin Elizabeth. The whole Church associates herself with these words.

We can say that the Rosary is, in a certain way, a prayerful commentary on the last chapter of the Constitution on the Church ("Lumen Gentium") of the Second Vatican Council, a chapter that treats the wonderful presence of the Mother of God in the mysteries of Christ and the Church.

THE RHYTHM OF HUMAN LIFE

O N the backdrop of the words "Hail Mary" the principal episodes of the life of Jesus Christ pass before the eyes of the soul.

These comprise the joyful, sorrowful, and glorious mysteries, and they place us in living communion with Jesus through the heart of His Mother.

At the same time, our heart can include in these decades of the Rosary all the events that comprise the life of the individual, the family, the nation, and all humankind: our own circumstances, those of our neighbor, and especially those of people who are closest to us, people who are dear to our heart.

Thus, the simple prayer of the Rosary beats out the rhythm of human life

MARY IS AT THE CORE OF OUR PRAYER

M ARY is always at the core of our prayer. She is the first among those who ask. And she is the "Omnipotentia supplex": the Omnipotence of intercession.

She was such a powerful interceder in her house at Nazareth when she spoke with Gabriel. We see her there deep in prayer. While she is deep in prayer, God the Father speaks to her. While she is deep in prayer, the Eternal Word becomes her Son. While she is deep in prayer, the Holy Spirit descends upon her.

Then Mary transfers this profundity of prayer from Nazareth to the Upper Room of Pentecost, where all the Apostles—Peter and John, James and Andrew, Philip and Thomas, Bartholomew and Matthew, James of Alphaeus and Simon the Zealot party member, and Jude of James—were together with her assiduous and united in prayer (cf. Acts 1:13).

THE ROSARY, OUR FAVORITE PRAYER

THE prayer that Mary says with the Apostles in the Upper Room is called the Rosary. And it is our favorite prayer, the prayer we direct to her, Mary. Certainly. But let us not forget that at the same time "the Rosary is our prayer in unison with Mary." It is Mary's prayer in unison with us, with the successors of the Apostles, who have constituted the beginning of the new Israel, the new People of God.

Hence, we come to pray here with Mary; to meditate with her on the mysteries which as a Mother she meditated on in her heart (cf. Lk 2:19) and continues to meditate on and to consider. For these are the "mysteries" of eternal life. They all possess their eschatological dimension. They are all "immersed in God Himself." In that God Who "dwells in unapproachable light" (1 Tm 6:16) are immersed all these Mysteries, which are so simple and so "accessible"—and so closely connected with the history of our salvation.

MARY'S PRAYER IS OPEN TO THE EARTH

MARY'S prayer, immersed in the light of God Himself, remains at the same time "ever open to the earth." To all human problems. To the problems of every person and also all human communities, families, and nations; and to the international problems of humankind.

This prayer of Mary, this Rosary, is constantly open "to the whole mission of the Church," to her difficulties and her hopes, to persecutions and incomprehensions, to every service that she carries out in favor of individuals and peoples.

GOD AMONG US

THIS prayer of Mary, this Rosary, is precisely that type of prayer because from the beginning it has been pervaded by the "logic of the heart."

And the prayer has been formed in Mary's heart through the most splendid experience that she has participated in: through the mystery of the Incarnation.

God had already given us a sign about this event: "The virgin shall be with Child, and bear a Son, and shall name Him Emmanuel" (Is 7:14). Emmanuel, "which means, 'God is with us' " (Mt 1:23). With us and for us: "to gather into one all the dispersed children of God" (Jn 11:52).

WE PENETRATE INTO
THE MYSTERIES OF JESUS' LIFE

I WANT to take a look at "the simplicity and, at the same time, the profundity" of this prayer, to which the Mother most holy in a special way invites us, inspires us, and encourages us.

By reciting the Rosary, we penetrate into the mysteries of Jesus' life, which are at the same time the mysteries of His Mother.

This is especially noticeable in the "joyful mysteries," beginning with the Annunciation, passing through the Visitation and the Birth of Jesus on the night of Bethlehem, and then through the Presentation of the Lord and on to the Finding in the Temple when Jesus was twelve.

MARY PARTICIPATES IN
THE LIFE OF HER SON

ADMITTEDLY, it may appear that the "sorrowful" mysteries do not directly show us the Mother of Jesus—with the exception of the last two: the Carrying of the Cross and the Crucifixion. However, can we really think that the Mother was not spiritually present when her Son was suffering so terribly in Gethsemani, at the Scourging, and at the Crowning with Thorns?

And the "glorious" mysteries are also mysteries of Christ in which we find the "spiritual presence" of Mary, above all the mystery of the Resurrection.

In speaking of the Ascension, Sacred Scripture does not mention Mary's presence. But could it be that she was not there when directly afterward we read that she was present in the Upper Room with the same Apostles who said farewell to Christ ascending into heaven?

In unison with them Mary prepares for the coming of the Holy Spirit and participates in the Pentecost of His Descent.

OUR BEST MEDIATRIX

THE last two glorious mysteries direct our thoughts precisely to the Mother of God, when we contemplate her Assumption and her Crowning in heavenly glory.

The Rosary is a prayer "concerning Mary" united with Christ in His salvific mission. At the same time it is a prayer "to Mary"—our best mediatrix with her Son.

Finally, it is a prayer that in a special way we recite "with Mary," as the Apostles in the Upper Room prayed with her, preparing themselves to receive the Holy Spirit.

COURAGEOUS COMBATANTS

I WISH to direct my thought to a prayer that is so dear to the hearts of Catholics, so loved by me, and so recommended by the Popes who were my predecessors.

Even the Rosary has taken on new perspectives and assumed more profound and more vast intentions than in the past.

Nowadays, it is not a question of asking Mary for great victories but of asking her to make us courageous combatants against the spirit of error and evil, with the arms of the Gospel, which are the Cross and the Word of God.

THE PRAYER OF PEOPLE FOR PEOPLE

THE prayer of the Rosary is the prayer of people for people. It is the prayer of human solidarity, the collegial prayer of the redeemed, which reflects the spirit and intentions of the first redeemed person, Mary, Mother and image of the Church. It is the prayer for all human beings in the world and in history, living or dead, called to be in the Body of Christ and to become with Him coheirs of the glory of the Father.

Considering the spiritual orientations suggested by the Rosary, a simple and evangelical prayer (cf. MC 46), we rediscover the intentions that St. Cyprian noted in the Our Father. He wrote: "The Lord, teacher of peace and unity, did not desire that we should pray individually and by ourselves. We do not say: 'My Father, Who art in heaven,' nor do we say: 'Give me my daily bread.'

"Our prayer is for all, so that when we pray we do not pray for only one person but for the whole people, because we constitute a single thing with the whole people."

THE HIGHEST EXPRESSION
OF HUMANKIND AT PRAYER

THE Rosary is addressed with insistence to the one who is the highest expression of humankind at prayer, model of the Church praying and requesting, in Christ, the mercy of the Father. Just as Christ "forever lives to make intercession" for us (Heb 7:25), so Mary continues in heaven her mission as Mother and becomes the voice of every person for every person, until the definitive crowning of the members of the elect (cf. LG 62).

In praying to her, we ask her to assist us throughout the entire course of our present life and above all at the decisive moment for our eternal destiny, which will be "the hour of our death."

The Rosary is a prayer that indicates the Kingdom of God and orients people to receive the fruits of the Redemption.

"SHE WAS DEEPLY TROUBLED"

"SHE was deeply troubled . . . and wondered what his greeting meant."

Luke the Evangelist says that Mary was "deeply troubled" by the words that the Archangel Gabriel addressed to her at the moment of the Annunciation and "wondered what his greeting meant" (Lk 1:29).

This meditation on Mary's part constitutes the first model of the prayer of the Rosary. It is the prayer of those who love the Angel's salutation to Mary.

Those who recite the Rosary take up again in their thought and in their heart the meditation of Mary, and while reciting it they meditate on what such a greeting means.

"THE LORD IS WITH YOU"

ABOVE all, "they repeat the words" addressed to Mary by God Himself through His messenger. Those who love the Angel's salutation to Mary repeat the words "that come" from God. In reciting the Rosary, we say those words many times. This is not a simplistic recitation.

The words addressed to Mary by God Himself and pronounced by the Divine messenger possess "an inscrutable content."

"Hail Mary, full of grace, the Lord is with you . . ." (Lk 1:28), "blessed are you among women" (Lk 1:42).

THE MYSTERY OF THE REDEMPTION

THIS content is "closely connected with the mystery of the Redemption." The words of the Angel's salutation to Mary introduce us into this mystery and at the same time find their explanation in it.

This is expressed by the reading from the Book of Genesis.

It is precisely then—with the backdrop of the first sin, the original sin—that "God announces for the first time" the mystery of the Redemption.

For the first time He reveals His action in the future history of humankind and of the world.

"HE SHALL CRUSH YOUR HEAD"

TO the tempter who hides beneath the guise of a serpent, the Creator says: "I will put enmity between you and the Woman, and between your offspring and hers; He will crush your head, while you strike at His heel" (Gn 3:15).

The words that Mary heard at the Annunciation reveal that "the time for the fulfillment of the promise" contained in the Book of Genesis has come. From the protoevangelium we pass on to the Gospel itself. The mystery of the Redemption is about to be accomplished.

The message of the eternal God salutes the "Woman": this Woman is Mary of Nazareth. She is saluted in consideration of the "Stock" that she will receive from God Himself: "The Holy Spirit will come upon you and the power of the Most High will overshadow you. . . . You shall conceive and bear a Son, and you shall give Him the Name Jesus" (Lk 2:35, 31).

THE MYSTERY THAT FILLS ETERNITY

THE Angel's salutation to Mary constitutes the beginning of the greatest "works of God" in the history of the human race and the world. This greeting provides a closeup view of the perspective of the Redemption.

It is not surprising that Mary, upon hearing the words of such a greeting, remained "deeply troubled." "The approach of the living God" always stirs up " a holy fear." Neither is it surprising that Mary wondered "what the greeting meant."

The words of the Archangel "have brought her" face to face with an inscrutable Divine mystery. Even more, they have inserted her within the orbit of that mystery.

It is not enough simply to take note of this mystery. We must meditate on it ever anew and ever more deeply. It has the power "to fill not only life but also eternity."

ON THE THRONE OF DAVID

ALL of us who love the Angel's salutation strive to "participate" in the meditation of Mary.

We strive to do this above all when we recite the Rosary.

In the words unttered by the Messenger at Nazareth, Mary as it were foresees, in God, "her whole life" on earth and in eternity.

Why is it that on learning that she is to become the Mother of the Son of God, she responds not with spiritual transports but first of all with the "humble fiat" ("let it be done" or "yes"): "Behold, I am the servant of the Lord. Let it be done to me as you say" (Lk 1:38)?

Is it not perhaps right from that moment that she experienced "the piercing sorrow of that rule" "over the throne of David" that would be proper to Jesus?

HIS REIGN WILL BE WITHOUT END

THE Archangel announces that "His reign will be without end."

Through the words of the angelic salutation to Mary there begin to be revealed all the mysteries in which the world's Redemption will be accomplished: the joyful, the sorrowful, and the glorious mysteries, as occurs in the Rosary.

Mary, who "wondered what [the Angel's] greeting meant," seems to enter into all of these mysteries, introducing us too into them.

She introduces us into the mysteries of Christ and at the same time into her own mysteries. Her act of meditation at the moment of the Annunciation "paves the way for our meditation" during and as a result of the recitation of the Rosary.

LIKE THE APOSTLES IN THE UPPER ROOM

THE Rosary is the prayer by which, through the repetition of the Angel's salutation to Mary, we seek to draw from the meditation of the Blessed Virgin our considerations concerning the mystery of the Redemption.

This reflection—begun at the moment of the Annunciation—continues in the glory of the Assumption.

In eternity Mary, profoundly immersed in the mystery of the Father, the Son, and the Holy Spirit, "unites herself" as our Mother "to the prayer" of those who love the Angel's salutation and express it in the recitation of the Rosary.

In this prayer, "we unite ourselves to Mary like the Apostles gathered together in the Upper Room after Christ's Ascension.

The author of the Acts of the Apostles—after mentioning the names of the individual Apostles—writes: "Together they devoted themselves to constant prayer. There were some women in the company, and Mary the Mother of Jesus, and His brothers" (Acts 1:14).

MARY PRESIDES OVER OUR PRAYER

WITH prayer the Apostles prepared themselves to receive the Holy Spirit on the day of Pentecost.

Mary, who on the day of the Annunciation had obtained "the Holy Spirit in an eminent fullness," prayed with them.

The special fullness of the Holy Spirit in Mary also includes a special "fullness of prayer."

Through this singular fullness, Mary prays "for us"—and she prays "with us."

In motherly fashion, she presides over our prayer. She brings together all over the earth the immense company of those who love the Angel's salutation: "in unison with her," they "meditate on" the mystery of the world's redemption by reciting the Rosary.

In this way, the Church continually prepares herself to receive the Holy Spirit, as on the day of Pentecost.

"THE SWEET CHAIN THAT BINDS YOU TO GOD"

POPE Leo XIII in the encyclical "Supremi apostolatus" (Supreme apostolate) decreed that the month of October should be especially dedicated to the cult of Our Lady of the Rosary.

In this document the Pope strongly emphasized the extraordinary effectiveness of this prayer when it is recited with a pure and devout spirit for the purpose of obtaining—from the Heavenly Father, in Christ, and through the intercession of the Mother of God—protection against the greatest evils that can threaten Christianity and humankind itself and in this way obtaining the supreme goods of justice and peace among individuals and among peoples.

With this historic action, Leo XIII did nothing else but join the ranks of numerous Pontiffs who had preceded him—among them St. Pius V—and he left to those who were to succeed him a legacy to promote the practice of the Rosary.

That is why I too wish to say to all of you: make the Rosary the "sweet chain that binds you to God" through Mary.

HAVE RECOURSE TO THE MOTHER OF GOD

ALL of us have recourse with great affection to the "Mother of God," repeating the words of the Archangel Gabriel: "Hail, full of grace, the Lord is with you"; "blessed are you among women."

And from the heart of today's Liturgy we hear "Mary's response": "My soul proclaims the greatness of the Lord, my spirit rejoices in God my Savior, for He has looked upon His servant in her lowliness; all ages to come shall call me blessed."

THE CONTEMPLATIVE ELEMENTS OF THE ROSARY

THE Holy Rosary is a continous memorial of the Redemption, in its salient stages: the Incarnation of the Word, His Passion and Death for us, the Pasch that He has begun and that will be completed eternally in heaven.

Indeed, when we consider the contemplative elements of the Rosary, that is, the mysteries around which the vocal prayer unfolds, we can better understand why this crown of "Aves" has been termed "the Psalter of the Virgin."

The Psalms reminded Israel of the wonders of the Exodus and of the salvation worked by God, and they constantly called the people back to fidelity toward the pact made at Sinai. In like manner, the Rosary continually reminds the people of the New Covenant of the prodigies of mercy and power that God has deployed in Christ on behalf of humankind, and it calls that people back to fidelity toward commitments made at Baptism.

We are His people and He is our God.

ITINERARY TOWARD THE PROMISED LAND

THIS reminder of the works of God and this constant summons to fidelity pass, in a certain way, through Mary, the faithful Virgin.

The succession of "Aves" helps us to penetrate, from time to time, even more profoundly into the supreme mystery of the incarnate and saving Word (cf. LG 65), "through the eyes of her who was closest to the Lord" (MC 47).

For even Mary, as the Daughter of Zion and heir of the sapiential spirituality of Israel, has chanted the prodigies of the Exodus; but as the first and most perfect disciple of Christ, she has preceded and lived in advance the Pasch of the New Covenant, guarding in her heart and meditating on her Son's every word and every action, associating herself with Him in unconditional fidelity, indicating to all the path of the new pact: "Do whatever He tells you" (Jn 2:5).

Now glorified in heaven, she points out the itinerary that has been accomplished in her, the itinerary of the new people toward the Promised Land.

THE PRAYER THAT UPLIFTS US

T HE Holy Rosary is an evangelical and ecclesial Christian prayer, but it is also a prayer that elevates the sentiments and affections of human beings.

In the joyful mysteries, over which we briefly pause today, we see a little of all this: the joy of the family, of motherhood, of parenthood, of friendship, and of mutual aid.

These joys, which sin has not completely snuffed out, have been taken up by Christ and made holy. He has done this through Mary.

Hence, it is through her that we can gather together and make our own all the joys of humankind. These are simple and lowly in themselves, but in Mary and Jesus they become great and holy.

A CHILD THAT BELONGS TO GOD

I N Mary virginally espoused to Joseph and Divinely fecundated is found the joy of chaste love of spouses and of motherhood welcomed and preserved as a gift of God. In Mary who out of loving concern goes to visit Elizabeth is found the joy of serving others by bringing them the presence of God. In Mary who presents the Hope of Israel to the shepherds and the Magi is found the spontaneous and confident sharing proper to friendship.

In Mary who in the Temple offers her Son to the Eternal Father is found the anguish-tinged joy proper to parents and educators toward their children or their students. In Mary who after three days of agonizing search recovers Jesus is found the joy united with suffering of the mother who knows that her child belongs to God before belonging to her.

IN THE ROSARY WE RELIVE THE HOPES OF CHRISTIANS

IN the glorious mysteries of the Holy Rosary, we relive the hopes of Christians: the hopes of eternal life, which engage God's omnipotence, and the hopes of the present time, which engage human beings to collaborate with God.

In Christ Who rises again, the whole world rises again inaugurating a new heavens and a new earth, which will be completed upon His glorious return when "there shall be no more death or mourning, crying out or pain, because the former world has passed away" (Rv 21:4).

In Christ Who ascends into heaven, human nature is exalted and placed at God's right hand, and the mandate to evangelize the earth is given to the disciples. Moreover, in rising to heaven, Christ has not vanished from the earth; He has hidden Himself beneath the countenance of every person, especially the most disadvantaged: the poor, the sick, the ostracized, and the persecuted.

TO HONOR THE MOTHER

BY sending forth the Holy Spirit at Pentecost, Christ has given the disciples the power to love and to spread His truth, He has requested communion in building a world worthy of redeemed people, and He has granted the ability for sanctifying all things in obedience to the will of the Heavenly Father.

In this way, Christ has rekindled the joy of giving in the soul of those who give, and He has rekindled the certainty of being loved in the heart of the disadvantaged.

In the glory of the Assumption of the Virgin Mary, the first among the redeemed, we contemplate among other things the true sublimation of the ties of blood and of family affections. For Christ has glorified Mary not only because she is immaculate and the ark of the Divine Presence but also because as a Son He wanted to honor His Mother.

GOD IS LOVE

THE sacred ties of earth are not dissolved in heaven. On the contrary, in the solicitude of the

Virgin Mother assumed into heaven to become our Advocate and Protectrix and a type of the victorious Church, we discover the very model who inspired the concerned love of our dearly departed for us, a love not effaced by death but rendered more powerful in the light of God.

Finally, in the vision of Mary glorified by all creatures we celebrate the eschatological mystery of a humankind reconstructed by Christ into perfect unity, with no more divisions and no other rivalry but to outdo one another in love. For God is Love.

In the mysteries of the Rosary, therefore, we contemplate and relive the joys, sorrows, and glories of Christ and of His holy Mother, which become the joys, sorrows, and hopes of humankind.

THE ROSARY INSPIRES JOYOUS FAITH

"BLESSED is she who has believed." These words, addressed to Mary by Elizabeth during the Visitation, "pervade our prayer of the Rosary"—especially during the month of October, which is the month of the Rosary.

In reciting each "decade," we meditate on the joyful, sorrowful, and glorious mysteries one after the other, and in each of them we say to Mary, as Elizabeth said during the Visitation, "Blessed is she who has believed."

"THE MYSTERIES" OF THE ROSARY

YOU, O Mary, believed, with a faith full of joy: at the Annunciation, Visitation, Nativity, Presentation in the Temple, and Finding in the Temple.

You believed with a faith full of sorrow: during the whole Agony in Gethsemani, the Scourging, the Crowning with Thorns, the Way of the Cross; and you believed at the Foot of the Cross on Calvary.

You believed with "the faith of an incipient glory, at the glorification" of your Son: at the Resurrection, at the Ascension, and on the day of Pentecost. Your faith was completed at the Assumption: you are our Mother, adorned with the crown of heavenly glory!

This is how we pray to Mary as we recite the Holy Rosary. We thank her in a special way for "the faith of the martyrs," for the faith of the whole Church in the course of the last two centuries.

We also thank her for the faith attested to "by missionaries," some of whom are among the ranks of the martyrs.

And we say: "Blessed are those who have believed unto the shedding of blood!"

QUEEN OF ALL SAINTS

"BLESSED are you among women. The Holy Spirit will come upon you and the power of the Most High will overshadow you" (Lk 1:42, 35).

In you we desire to adore God to the highest possible degree, for the gift of holiness offered to human beings in Jesus Christ.

Be pleased to preside over our prayer for the dead with which the Church, in a certain sense, completes the joy of the solemnity of All Saints.

ENTRUSTING TO MARY THE FATE OF THE CHURCH

THE jubilation with which the people of Ephesus, in that distant 431, welcomed the Fathers emerging from the Council hall where the true faith of the Church had been reaffirmed quickly spread to every part of the Christian world. And since that time the jubilation has not ceased to resound among successive generations who in the course of the centuries have continued to have recourse with total confidence to Mary, as to one who has given life to the Son of God.

We too, with the same filial love and the same intense trust, have recourse to the Blessed Virgin, greeting in her the "Mother of God" and entrusting to her the fate of the Church, which is subjected in these times to singularly harsh and insidious trials but is also inspired by the action of the Spirit along ways that are open to the most promising hopes.

THE INEFFABLE MOMENT
OF THE INCARNATION

"MOTHER of God." In repeating this term charged with mystery, we go back in spirit to the ineffable moment of the Incarnation and we affirm with the whole Church that the Virgin became Mother of God because she gave birth in the flesh to a Son Who was personally the Word of God. What an abyss of condescension opens up before us!

A question immediately occurs to the thoughtful person: Why did the Word prefer to be born of a woman (Gal 4:4) rather than to descend from heaven with a fully formed adult body, fashioned by God's hand (cf. Gn 2:7)? Would this not have been a way more worthy of Him—one more worthy of His mission as Master and Savior of the human race?

THE MISSION OF THE YOUNG
WOMAN OF NAZARETH

WE know that especially in the first few centuries not a few Christians (Docetists, Gnostics, and the like) would have preferred that things had been done the second way mentioned above. However, the Word chose the first way. Why?

The answer comes to us with the clear and convincing simplicity of the works of God.

Christ wished to be a true shoot (cf. Is 11:1) of the trunk He was coming to save. He desired that the

Redemption should spring forth, so to speak, from the interior of humankind, as something of its own.

Christ wanted to help human beings not as a stranger but as a brother, making Himself like them in all things except sin (cf. Heb 4:15). That is why He wanted a Mother—and He found one in Mary.

The fundamental mission of the young woman of Nazareth was, therefore, that of being the Savior's means of union with the human race.

MARY RECEIVED THE WORD OF GOD IN HER HEART

IN the History of Salvation, the action of God does not occur without a call for the collaborative effort of human beings. God does not impose salvation. And He did not impose it on Mary.

In the Annunciation, He turned to Mary in a personal way, asked for her willingness, and awaited a response that came from her faith.

The Fathers have gone into this aspect in depth, stressing that "the Blessed Virgin Mary by believing in the One Whom she bore also conceived Him in an act of faith."

The Second Vatican Council stressed the same point by affirming that "at the message of the Angel, the Virgin Mary received the Word of God in her heart as well as in her body" (LG 53).

Thus, the "fiat" ("let it be done" or "yes") of the Annunciation inaugurates the New Covenant be-

tween God and the creature: while it incorporates
Jesus into our race according to nature, it incorporates Mary into Him according to grace. The bond
between God and humankind that was broken by
sin is now happily restored.

THE CONSENT
OF THE SERVANT OF GOD

THE complete and unconditional consent of "the
servant of the Lord" (Lk 1:38) to the design of
God was thus a free and conscious adherence.

Mary consented to become the Mother of the Messiah, Who had come "to save His people from their
sins" (Mt 1:21).

It was not a question of a simple consent to the
birth of Jesus but of the responsible acceptance of
participation in the work of salvation that He was
coming to accomplish.

The words of the "Magnificat" offer clear confirmation of this lucid awareness: "He has upheld Israel His servant," says Mary, "ever mindful of His
mercy; even as He promised our fathers, promised
Abraham and his descendants forever" (Lk 1:54f).

EARTHLY MOTHER
OF THE SON OF GOD

IN uttering her "fiat" ("let it be done" or "yes"),
not only does Mary become the Mother of the His-

torical Christ but her act makes her the Mother of the Total Christ, "Mother of the Church."

"From the moment of the 'fiat,' " observes St. Anselm, Mary began to bear all of us in her womb; that is why "the birth of the Head is also the birth of the Body," proclaims St. Leo the Great.

For his part, St. Ephrem has a very beautiful expression on the subject: "Mary," he says, is "the field in which the Church has been sown."

Indeed, at the moment when the Virgin becomes the Mother of the Word incarnate, the Church is constituted, in a secret but germinally perfect manner, in her essence as Mystical Body: for there are present the Redeemer and the first among the redeemed.

Henceforth, incorporation into Christ will involve a filial relationship not only with the Heavenly Father but also with Mary, the earthly Mother of His Son.

THE RESEMBLANCE BETWEEN MARY AND THE CHURCH

EVERY mother transmits her likeness to her children. Hence, between Mary and the Church there is a relationship of profound resemblance. Mary is the ideal figure, the prefiguration, the archetype of the Church.

She is the first among the lowly and the poor who have remained faithful and await the Redemption.

She is also the first among the redeemed who in humility and obedience welcome the coming of the Redeemer.

Eastern theology has greatly insisted on the "katharsis" (purification) that is worked in Mary at the moment of the Annunciation; it is sufficient for us to recall the moving paraphrase that the Orthodox bishop Gregory Palamas gives in a homily: "You are already holy and full of grace, O Virgin, says the Angel to Mary. But the Holy Spirit will come anew upon you, preparing you by an increase of grace for the Divine mystery."

THE MOST PERFECT IMAGE OF THE CHURCH

IN the Liturgy with which the Eastern Church celebrates the praises of the Virgin, a place of honor is justly accorded to the canticle that the sister of Moses, Miriam, chants after the passage through the Red Sea, as if to indicate that the Blessed Mother was the first to cross the sea of sin at the head of the new People of God, liberated by Christ.

Mary is the first and the most perfect image of the Church: "a most excellent part, a most remarkable part, a most chosen part." "She is one with all human beings in their need for salvation," proclaims the Second Vatican Council, and she has been "redeemed in an especially sublime manner by reason of the merits of her Son" (LG 53).

Hence, Mary stands before every believer as the all-pure, all-beautiful, all-holy creature capable of "being the Church" in a way that no other creature will ever be here on earth.

GROWTH IN FAITH

WE look to Mary with loving transports of children, as to our model. We look to her to learn from her example how to build the Church.

To this end, we know that we must first of all grow under her guidance in the exercise of our faith. Mary lived her faith in an attitude of continual deepening and progressive discovery, passing through difficult moments of darkness, right from the first days of her Motherhood (cf. Mt 1:18ff), which she overcame by a responsible attitude of listening and obedience in encounters with the Word of God.

We too must make every effort to deepen and consolidate our faith, "listening to, welcoming, proclaiming, venerating the Word of God, scrutinizing the signs of the times in its light, and interpreting and living the events of history."

EXAMPLE OF COURAGEOUS HOPE

MARY stands before us as an example of courageous hope and operative charity. She journeyed in hope, passing with docile promptness from the Jewish hope to Christian hope, and she activated her charity, welcoming in herself all its exigencies up to the most complete gift and the greatest sacrifice.

Faithful to her example, we too must remain unwavering in our hope even when storm clouds gather over the Church, which advances like a ship amidst the waves of human events that are often opposed to her. We too must grow in charity, cultivating humility, poverty, openness, and the capacity to listen and pay attention while adhering to what she has taught us through the testimony of her whole life.

OPENNESS TO THE SPIRIT

AS we stand at the feet of our common Mother, we wish to assume the commitment of one thing in particular. We want to commit ourselves to advancing—with all our energies and in an attitude of complete openness to the inspirations of the Spirit—along the path that leads to the perfect unity of all Christians.

Before her motherly eyes we are ready to acknowledge our mutual wrongs, our egoisms, and our tardinesses.

We entrust to Mary the sincere resolve not to give ourselves any peace until the goal is happily reached.

We seem to hear from her lips the words of the Apostle: "Let there not be among you discord, jealousy, animosity, factions, slander, gossip, arrogance, or disorder" (2 Cor 12:20).

Let us embrace this admonishment of hers with an open heart and let us ask her to be with us to guide us, with a gentle but firm hand, along the paths of full and lasting fraternal understanding.

MARY AIDS US

IN the providential plan of Creation and the Redemption, the Lord has willed to place the Blessed Virgin Mary by our side. She stands beside us, she exhorts us, and by her spirituality she shows us where are found the light and strength that will enable us to follow the path of life.

While still a young man, Father Maximilian Kolbe was already writing his mother from Rome in this fashion: "How many times in life I have experienced the special protection of the Immaculata . . . ! I place in her all my hope for the future."

WELCOME THE FATHER'S CALL

IN the presence of the Archangel Gabriel who announced God's call and her own specific and extraordinary vocation to become the Mother of the Messiah, of the Savior Jesus, Mary accepted without hesitation: "Behold, I am the servant of the Lord. Let it be done to me as you say" (Lk 1:38).

Just as decisive and deep must be the Christian faith in God that works everything in us. We are struck by the words that we have just heard in the Gospel: "No one can come to Me unless the Father Who sent Me draws him. . . . Everyone who has heard the Father and learned from Him comes to Me" (Jn 6:44f).

Behold: the power to know, follow, and love Jesus Christ is a special "call" from God. The saddest response is to refuse it. The most logical and sublime response is to accept the call with joy and thanks, and to live it with full and total adherence, as the Blessed Virgin did.

THE SPIRITUALITY OF MARY

"THE spirituality of Mary is one of total intimacy with Jesus": an organic intimacy that only the Mother can have, the one who has given physical life to Jesus, in a wondrous and spiritual way. This was an affective intimacy, because Jesus was her supreme and absolute love, from the Annunciation to Calvary, from the Resurrection to her Assumption into heaven. It was also an apostolic intimacy, because she united herself to Christ's redemptive work and even now she intervenes for all humankind.

May such an intimacy with Jesus be the fundamental characteristic of your life, an intimacy that is realized in an eminent and unique way in the Eucharist.

"I am the Bread of Life. . . . I am the living Bread come down from heaven."

Jesus Himself willed to have this mysterious and sublime intimacy with you through the Eucharist. And this Eucharistic intimacy is the principal means for attaining eternal life, which was promised us by Jesus.

It is my prayer that, following Mary's example, you will forever live this intimacy with Jesus.

FOLLOW THE WAY OF LOVE

MARY most holy gave herself completely to God and to Jesus. In the same way she also gave herself to the Apostles and disciples, to the needy, and to the Church that was being born, for whom she offered and continues to offer her secret and powerful services.

May the same be true of you: consecrate yourselves to charity! Where unfortunately there is hatred, bring love! Where there is war, bring peace!

As St. Paul says in his Letter to the Ephesians: "Be kind to one another, compassionate, and mutually forgiving. . . . Follow the way of love, even as Christ loved you" (Eph 4:32—5:2).

MARY IN THE LITURGY

TODAY I want to speak with you about the presence of the Blessed Virgin in the celebration of the Liturgy.

As you know, every liturgical action—and especially the celebration of the Eucharist—is an event of communion and a source of unity.

Every liturgical action is a communion with God: Father, Son, and Holy Spirit. Indeed, in the sacred action there comes to us the energy of the Spirit Who, as the river of life, springs forth from the eternal Liturgy, celebrated by the Risen Christ for the glory of God and the salvation of souls.

Every liturgical action is the communion of the heavenly Jerusalem with the Church still on pilgrimage along the paths of this world. In the celebration of the holy Mysteries, heaven and earth unite, are illumined by the same light, are aflame with the same charity, participate in the same life, and are founded on unity.

Every liturgical action is a communion among ourselves. In the Liturgy we profess the same faith, we participate in the same hope, and we are animated by the same love. Moved by the same Spirit, we invoke the same Father, and, as table companions of Christ, we are nourished by the same Word, the same Bread, and the same Chalice of life.

INTIMATELY UNITED WITH CHRIST AND THE CHURCH

THE communion of Christians [through the Liturgy] is also in a special way a communion with the Mother, the humble and glorious Mary.

Why? Because the Liturgy is an action of Christ and of the Church.

It is an action of Christ because He is the unique, the true, and the supreme priest (cf. Heb 8:1). Beneath the veil of sacred signs, it is He Who offers the Sacrifice, baptizes, and remits sins, places His hand on the sick, proclaims the Good News, praises and glorifies the Father, and offers prayers and intercessions for all human beings

It is an action of the Church because "Christ always associates the Church with Himself in the great work wherein God is perfectly glorified and human beings are sanctified. The Church is His beloved Bride who calls to her Lord and through Him offers worship to the Eternal Father" (SC 7).

Now, the Blessed Virgin is intimately united both with Christ and with the Church, and she is inseparable from one and the other. Hence, she is united with them in what constitutes the very essence of the Liturgy: the sacramental celebration of salvation for the glory of God and the sanctification of human beings.

THE PRESENCE OF MARY

MARY is present in the memorial—the liturgical action—because she was present at the salvific event.

She is present at every baptismal font, where in faith and in the Spirit the members of the Mystical

Body are born to Divine life, for by faith and the power of the Spirit she conceived their Divine Head, Christ.

She is present at every altar, where the memorial of the Passion-Resurrection is celebrated, because she was present—clinging with her whole being to the design of God—at the historico-salvific event of the death of Christ.

She is present at every cenacle (Upper Room), where by the imposition of hands and the holy anointing the Spirit is imparted to the faithful, because she was present at the Pentecostal effusion of the Spirit.

With both Christ, the High Priest, and the Church, the community of worship, Mary is continually united—in the salvific event and in its liturgical memorial. And Mary must also be present in the life of every Christian through a sincere and profound Marian devotion.

THE REIGN OF MARY

A FTER the example of her Divine Son, Mary is the "Queen" not of this world but of the Kingdom of God, which begins to grow here below as an ecclesial reality and is to be completed in the heavenly Jerusalem.

To this end, the "reign" of Mary, like that of Jesus, is not some ephemeral power often based on injustice and oppression, but it is—as St. Paul declares—"justice, peace, and the joy that is given by the Holy Spirit" (Rm 14:17).

The Virgin in the icon known as the "Hodege-tria" points with her hand to her Divine Son. She thus indicates to us the "way" to this Kingdom, because Jesus is precisely the Way. At the same time, she also indicates to us the "way" to unity among Christians, which consists in submitting ourselves, with absolute purity of intention and fervent coherence of life, to the spiritual royalty of Jesus and Mary.

DAUGHTER OF ZION

THE Second Vatican Council also applies to Our Lady the title of "exalted Daughter of Zion" (LG 55). This is a title that owes its origin to the traditions of the Old Testament and to an expression that is distinctly Eastern in flavor.

Zion was the rock of ancient Jerusalem. King David had the Ark of the Covenant transported to this summit (cf. 2 Sm 6), and his son Solomon erected the Temple on it (cf. 2 Sm 24).

From then on the name Zion designated above all the mount of the Temple (Is 18:7). Zion was therefore like the heart of Jerusalem, the most sacred part of the Holy City, because the Lord dwelt there, in His house.

As such, the hill of Zion came to designate all of Jerusalem (Is 37:32), and even all of Israel (Is

46:13), which had its religious and political center in Jerusalem.

ECHO OF THE JOYFUL MESSAGE

MARY can be called "Daughter of Zion" insofar as in her person she culminates and concretizes the vocation of the ancient Jerusalem and the whole chosen people.

She is the flower of Israel that sprouted at the end of a lengthy itinerary, comprised of lights and shadows, during which God was preparing Israel to accept the Messiah.

In Mary of Nazareth, God realizes in advance the promises made to Abraham and his posterity.

According to many Scripture scholars, in the words of the Angel Gabriel to Mary we hear the echo of the joyful message that the Prophets had addressed to the Daughter of Zion.

Mary is invited to rejoice ("Rejoice, O full of Grace": Lk 1:28), because the Son of God will make His dwelling in her (Lk 1:31f). He will be King and Savior of the new house of Jacob (Lk 1:32b-33), which is the Church.

THE END POINT
OF THE OLD TESTAMENT

INSOFAR as she is the "Daughter of Zion," the Virgin Mary is therefore the end point of the Old Testament and the firstfruits of the Church.

Moreover, she is a permanent reminder of the ties that bind us to Abraham, "our father in faith," and to the people that has hoped and longed for the event of the Redemption.

She is also an admonition to the Church—new "Daughter of Zion"—to live in joy.

Christ, indeed, is with us, forever (Mt 28:20).

PRESERVED FROM THE OPPRESSION OF EVIL

THE eschatological Kingdom of Christ and God (cf. Col 1:13) will be accomplished when the Lord shall be all in all, after having destroyed the kingdom of Satan, sin, and death.

Nonetheless, the Kingdom of God is already present "in mystery" in history, and it is operative in those who accept it.

It is present in the reality of the Church, which is the sacrament of salvation and at the same time the mystery whose confines are known only to the mercy of the Father, Who desires to save all. The holiness of the Church here below is the prefiguration of the future fullness of the Kingdom.

The splendid descriptions of the Letter to the Colossians in regard to this Kingdom (Col 1:13) refer to all Christians, but especially to Mary, preserved completely from the oppression of evil.

FAITHFUL DISCIPLE OF THE WORD

"**H**E rescued us from the power of darkness and brought us into the Kingdom of His beloved Son" (Col 1:13). It is in Christ that the Kingdom of God has burst forth in history, and those who have accepted it have become participants in it: "Any who did accept Him He empowered to become children of God. These are they who believe in His Name" (Jn 1:12).

Mary, Mother of Christ and faithful disciple of the Word, has entered into the fullness of the Kingdom. Her whole existence as a creature beloved of the Lord "(Kecharitomené")" and animated by the Spirit is the concrete witness of and the prelude to the eschatological realities.

IMAGE AND FULFILLMENT OF THE KINGDOM

THE Virgin Mary, already the sign and anticipation of future goods in her earthly life, is now, in her glorified state by the side of Christ the Lord, the image and fulfillment of the Kingdom of God.

She is the first to follow Christ, "the firstfruits among many brothers and sisters," "the beginning of the new creation and Head of the Church" (cf. Col 1:18-20). She is the first one to inherit His glory.

The glorification of Mary, our sister, is the most splendid confirmation of the word of Scripture:

"With and in Christ Jesus He raised us up and gave us a place in the heavens" (Eph 2:6).

Mary's entry into the eschatological Kingdom of God is the pledge and guarantee of the participation of the whole Church, the Body of Christ, in the glory of her Lord.

MARY INTERCEDES FOR THE SALVATION OF THE WORLD

IN the community of the believers at prayer, Mary is present—not only at the origins of faith but at all times.

"Mary appears as such in the visit to the Mother of the Precursor, when she pours out her soul in expressions glorifying God, and expressions of humility, faith, and hope. This prayer is the Magnificat, Mary's prayer par excellence, the song of the Messianic times in which there mingles the joy of the ancient and the new Israel" (MC 18).

Mary appears as the Virgin in prayer at Cana and as the Virgin in prayer in the Upper Room. "We have here the prayerful presence of Mary in the early Church and in the Church throughout the ages, for, having been assumed into heaven, she has not abandoned her mission of intercession and salvation. The title Virgin in prayer also fits the Church, which day by day presents to the Father the needs of her children, 'praises the Lord unceasingly and intercedes for the salvation of the world' " (MC 18).

EVERYTHING HAS BEEN CREATED THROUGH HIM

I WISH to dwell on a few aspects of Marian devotion, that is, on the dedicated and filial love with which the disciples of Christ both in the East and in the West venerate Mary most holy. Such devotion is the result of an exultant "Christian experience" in the sense that it is rooted in the mystery of Christ and finds in that mystery its origin and its meaning, the reason for its development and the ultimate goal to which it tends by an inner dynamism.

"In the beginning was the Word; the Word was in God's presence, and the Word was God" (Jn 1:1), writes John in the prologue to his Gospel. And he adds: "Through Him all things came into being" (Jn 1:3). All things. Even Mary. Indeed, especially Mary, who after the Sacred Humanity of Christ, constitutes the summit of creation, the "glory of the universe," as the Liturgy salutes her.

THE ARK OF THE COVENANT

"FOR Him everything . . . was created" (Col 1:16), the Apostle Paul specifies. Even Mary. She was created for Him, so that she might be His holy "Mother" and in her virginal womb the Word might take on human nature; so that she might be His faithful disciple and in the treasury of a pure heart might preserve the word of life (cf. Lk 2:19, 51); the new "woman," placed next to Him, the new

Man, Redeemer of all human beings, that she might be the "ark" of an unbreakable Covenant; the "image" of the new People of God and the new Jerusalem; the first and already perfected "fruit" of the Redemption.

LOVING VENERATION

"IN Him . . ." and "for Him," the Scriptures tell us.

Therefore, everything in Mary is related to Christ, everything depends on Him, and everything is pervaded by His mystery.

From apostolic times, Christians contemplated Jesus, "Lord of glory" (cf. 1 Cor 2:8), and by searching the mystery of His Person—Son of God and, through Mary, Son of Man—they came to understand the "essential" role of Mary in the work of salvation.

Then by gradually reflecting on the indissoluble association of the Mother with the salvific events of Christ's Life, Death, and Resurrection, they came to have toward her an attitude of moving wonder, faithful respect, and loving veneration.

A GRACE-EVENT

AS we know, the "mystery of Christ," in which Marian devotion is rooted, has through the action of the Spirit been expressed in words and set down in Sacred Scripture as an announcement of salvation, and it is realized and celebrated in the sacred Liturgy as a grace-event.

Indeed, when we examine the ancient documentation and Sacred Tradition, we see clearly that Marian devotion finds its origin in meditation on the Bible and celebration of the Divine Mysteries.

This joyous discovery is spontaneously turned into a timorous wish: that our devotion toward the Mother of Jesus may remain ever anchored in this twofold, genuine, and refreshing source—the Word of God and the Sacred Liturgy.

THE VIRGIN'S VOICE
ON BEHALF OF HUMANKIND

I WISH to pursue the reflection on the presence of the Virgin in the liturgical celebration, action of Christ and of the Church, with which Mary is indissolubly united. The Church has an intimate conviction of this fact, which comes to her from faith and, so to speak, from experience.

The Church believes that the Blessed Virgin, assumed into heaven, is by the side of Christ, Who forever lives to make intercession for us (cf. Heb 7:25), and that the unceasing prayer of the Mother is united with the Divine supplication of the Son. In heaven, the voice of the Virgin has become a suppliant liturgy on behalf of human beings, her children, whom she contemplates in the light of God and whose necessities and travail she knows.

MARY ACCOMPANIES THE CHURCH TOWARD THE HOMELAND

THE Church possesses the experience—intimate, vital, and indeed one that has matured as a result of a centuries-old tradition of praying—of the active presence of the Blessed Virgin, the Angels, and the Saints in the Liturgy. And she translates this experience, incurred above all in liturgical prayer, into multiform expressions of devotion, among which I wish to recall the request for Mary's Motherly intercession and communion with her.

Within the framework of Christ's unique mediation, God the Father has willed that the motherly love of the Blessed Virgin should accompany the Church along the paths toward the homeland. Hence, the Church wishes to walk this path in the company of the Mother of the Lord, whose heart beats with the pure offering of self and exults in the canticle of thanksgiving to the Most High.

"THROUGH YOU JOY IS BORN"

IN the Churches of the Byzantine Rite there takes place a magnificent Marian liturgical celebration: the celebration of the "Akathistos," a famous hymn that for many centuries has been sung everywhere in honor of the Mother of God.

"Rejoice [O Mary]: through you joy is born; rejoice: through you sorrow is put to flight."

So begins that ancient hymn, the object of a proper liturgical feast. Indeed, the presence of the Virgin in the design of God is extended when there is extended the mystery of the Humanity of Christ, the living sacrament of the unity and salvation of the human race.

Wherever Christ radiates His salvific action, there too is present His Mother, who clothed Him with flesh and gave Him to the world.

GOD'S CLEMENCY
TOWARD HUMAN BEINGS

MARY is present at the mystery that was accomplished one day in her womb, constituting her the throne of God more resplendent than a throne of Angels. "Rejoice, O most holy throne of Him Who sits above the Cherubim."

She is present in the effusion of peace and pardon that God dispenses to the world: "Rejoice, O clemency of God toward human beings."

She is present in the mercy that continues to be poured out in copious manner in the grace that clothes us with light: "Rejoice, O field that produces an abundance of mercies."

She is present on the lips of the Apostles who proclaim the Word and in the witness of the Martyrs who go to their death for Christ: "Rejoice, O perennial voice of the Apostles"; "Rejoice, O indomitable ardor of the Martyrs."

THE FOUNT OF HOLY MARTYRS

MARY is present in the journey of faith that brings catechumens to Baptism and in the Sacraments that engender and nourish the Church: "Rejoice [O Mary]: you are the fount of the Holy Martyrs, you are the source of abundant Waters, you are the life of the sacred Banquet."

She is present in the pilgrimage of the Church toward the homeland of heaven, through the heart of the world. "Rejoice: through you we raise high our standards; rejoice: through you our enemies are vanquished."

She is present by the side of every one of us who trusts in her. "Rejoice: you are the medicine of my body; you are the salvation of my soul!"

MARY IS CONCERNED WITH THE THINGS OF THE LORD

MARY experienced the significance of being able to recognize the nearness of God. Mary is the Virgin whose love is not divided. She is concerned only with the things of the Lord, and she desires to follow Him alone in word and in deed (cf. 1 Cor 7:32-34).

At the same time, even Mary has a holy fear of God and she is "troubled" by the words of God's command. God has chosen and sanctified this Virgin as the dwelling place for His Eternal Word.

Mary, the exalted Daughter of Zion, experienced as no one else how close are "the power and greatness" of God. Full of joy and gratitude, she invokes Him in the Magnificat: "My soul proclaims the greatness of the Lord, my spirit rejoices in God my Savior. . . . God Who is mighty has done great things for me, and holy is His Name" (Lk 1:46-49).

At the same time, Mary is profoundly aware of her creaturehood: "He has looked upon His servant in her lowliness." She knows that all ages will call her blessed (cf. Lk 1:46-49); but she points us toward Jesus: "Do whatever He tells you" (Jn 2:5). She is concerned with the things of the Lord.

FOLLOW MARY IN HER PILGRIMAGE OF FAITH

IN her continually renewed self-offering to God, Mary "advanced in her pilgrimage of faith" (LG 58). The Virgin of Nazareth contemplated God's incomprehensible action with the eyes of faith.

Luke twice stresses that she "kept in her heart" what had occurred (cf. Lk 2:19, 51). A faith such as this is praised: "Blessed is she who has believed. . . ." (Lk 1:45).

Dear brothers and sisters, follow Mary in her pilgrimage of faith! Like her, open your hearts completely to the things of the Lord! I address this invitation to all: to bishops, priests, and deacons, to religious and laity, to men and women.

Unquestionably, there exists in all of us the deep and ardent desire of human beings to experience the living God. This desire has always called men and women to the commitment to follow Christ in faith.

"HERE I AM; SEND ME!"

THE person who seeks the community of believers, especially the person who draws close to Mary, enters the realm of the Spirit. Mary truly received from the Angel the promise of grace and the Spirit (Lk 1:28, 35). Like Mary, we want to be open to the Spirit of God, to be able to experience His might, which strengthens us for the service and the witness to which we are called.

Be concerned with the things of the Lord. Seek the holy God. I recall anew the vision of the Prophet Isaiah.

Isaiah's mission to human beings is rooted in the personal experience of a thrice-holy God. He is empowered to hear the voice of the Lord. He perceives the request to be open to the prophetic service. And he gives his acceptance to the mission that comes from on high: "Here I am; send me" (Is 6:8).

THE EXPERIENCE OF GOD'S NEARNESS

EVEN Mary had first to experience the nearness of the Lord: "The Lord is with you."

She received the promise of grace before being asked if she accepted her unique vocation, that of becoming the Mother of the Messiah. Then she gave her unqualified "Yes" for her collaboration in the salvific work of God: "Behold, I am the servant of the Lord. Let it be done to me as you say" (Lk 1:38).

Mary comes to a decision after reflection; but she does not pose conditions. She is ready to offer service because the holy God is near. With patience she advances in "the pilgrimage of faith" until she stands beneath her Son's Cross.

In this pilgrimage she is fully united with us: a compassionate sister and mother.

AT THE SERVICE OF HUMANKIND

THEREFORE, let us take as our model Mary, Mother of Jesus, who is also Mother of the Church and our Mother; let us also take her as our companion on our earthly exile.

In all the circumstances of our lives we wish to come apart with her in order to seek the holy God, Who is always diverse from and greater than we are, yet is ever close in a mysterious way and loves us. With our gaze fixed on this God. Who in Christ has become our Father, we too say: "Here I am; send me." "Let it be done to me as you say." For the service of God and for the salvation of human beings!

CONCERNED IN MOTHERLY FASHION FOR THE SALVATION OF ALL

PRAYER illumines and sustains the course of history and the destiny of our brothers and sisters! It is a sign of the solidarity of human beings and of the mutual aid they can offer one another when they are open to the designs of God!

But what creature is more open to the Lord than is Mary, His Mother and Handmaid? Who more than Mary continues in heaven to praise, adore, and implore the Lord? In the words of the Second Vatican Council, "taken up to heaven, she did not lay aside this salvific function, but by her manifold acts of intercession she continues to win for us gifts of eternal salvation" (LG 62).

Yes, Mary is the great Virgin in prayer, and she lifts up her hands in a gesture of openness to God and of universal supplication, concerned in a motherly fashion for the salvation of all.

Let us always remember that in heaven Mary prays for us, and let us therefore rely with confidence on her powerful intercession, with the desire that God's will may be done in us.

"WE FLY TO YOUR PATRONAGE, O HOLY MOTHER OF GOD"

"WE fly to your patronage,
O holy Mother of God."
In pronouncing the words of this anthem,

with which the Church of Christ has prayed for centuries,
we find ourselves before you,
Mother of our Redemption.

We are united
with all the Pastors of the Church,
in a special bond,
constituting a body and a college,
in the same way that through Christ's will
the Apostles constituted one body
and one college with Peter.

In the bond of unity,
we pronounce the words of the present Act
in which we desire to include
still once more
the hopes and fears of the Church
for the contemporary world.

THE WHOLE WORLD
CONSECRATED TO MARY

YEARS ago, your servant Pope Pius XII,
having before his eyes
the sad experience of the human family,
"entrusted and consecrated
to your Immaculate Heart"
the whole world
and especially the Peoples
who because of their situations
form the particular object of your love
and your concern.

We have before our eyes still today
"this world of individuals and nations":
the world of the second millennium
which is about to come to a close,
the contemporary world,
our world!

"MAKE DISCIPLES OF ALL THE NATIONS"

MINDFUL of the Lord's words:
"Go and make disciples of all the nations. . . .
Know that I am with you always
until the end of the world" (Mt 28:19f),
"the Church" has revitalized
in the Second Vatican Council
the consciousness of "her mission in this world."

And therefore,
O Mother of individuals and of peoples,
you who know all their sorrows
and their hopes,
you who share in maternal fashion
all the struggles between good and evil,
between light and darkness,
that shake the contemporary world,
heed the cry that moved by the Spirit,
we address directly to your Heart.

EMBRACE OUR WORLD, O MARY

WITH the "love of a Mother"
and of the Servant of the Lord,
embrace our human world,
which we entrust and consecrate to you,
out of deep concern
for the earthly and eternal lot
of its individuals and peoples.
In a special way, we entrust and consecrate to you
those individuals and those nations
who are particularly needful
of this consecration.

"We fly to your patronage,
O holy Mother of God!"
"Despise not our petitions
in our necessities."

Behold, finding ourselves before you,
O Mother of Christ,
before your Immaculate Heart,
we desire with the whole Church,
to unite ourselves to the consecration that,
for love of us,
your Son has made of Himself to the Father:
"I consecrate Myself for their sakes now,
that they may be consecrated in truth" (Jn 17:19).

BLESSED ABOVE ALL CREATURES

WE wish to unite ourselves
with our Redeemer
in this consecration
for the world and for individuals,
for in His Divine Heart
it has the power to obtain pardon
and to bring about reparation.

"The power of this consecration"
endures for all ages
and embraces all individuals, peoples, and nations.
It overcomes every evil
that the spirit of darkness
is capable of stirring up in human hearts
and in human history
and that he has in fact stirred up
in our day.

How deeply we feel the need of consecration
for humankind and for the world:
for our contemporary world
in union with Christ Himself!

Indeed, the world must participate in
Christ's redemptive work
through the Church.

May you be blessed "above every creature,"
O Servant of the Lord,

who in the fullest way
obeyed the Divine call!

May you be saluted
for "uniting yourself completely"
to your Son's redemptive consecration!

TEACH US THE PATHS OF FAITH

MOTHER of the Church,
teach the People of God
the paths of faith, hope, and charity!

Help us to live in the truth
of the consecration of Christ
for the entire human family
of the contemporary world.

Entrusting to you,
O Mother,
the world, all individuals, and all peoples,
we also entrust to you
the "consecration of the world,"
placing it in your Motherly Heart!

O Immaculate Heart,
help us to overcome the threat of evil,
which so easily takes root
in the hearts of people today
and which in its immeasurable effects
weighs heavily upon the present life
and seems to close the paths to the future!

ACT OF OFFERING

FROM hunger and war,
deliver us!
From nuclear war,
from an incalculable self-destruction,
from every kind of war,
deliver us!
From sins against human life
beginning with its first moments,
deliver us!
From the hatred for and the degradation of
the dignity of the children of God,
deliver us!
From every kind of injustice
in social, national, and international life,
deliver us!
From trampling with ease upon God's command-
ments,
deliver us!
From the attempt to obscure in human hearts
the very truth of God,
deliver us!
From the loss
of the consciousness of good and evil,
deliver us!
From sins against the Holy Spirit,
deliver us, deliver us!

THE LIGHT OF HOPE

HEED, O Mother of Christ,
this cry "charged with the suffering"
of all human beings!
"Charged with the suffering"
of entire societies!

Help us by the power of the Holy spirit
to overcome every sin:
the sin of individuals
and the "sin of the world,"
sin in every one of its manifestations.

Let there be revealed once more,
in the history of the world,
the infinite salvific power of the Redemption:
the power "of merciful Love!"

May it arrest evil
and transform consciences!

In your Immaculate Heart
let the light of Hope
be manifested to all human beings!

ABBREVIATIONS OF BOOKS OF THE BIBLE

Acts	— Acts of the Apostles	Jl	— Joel
Am	— Amos	Jn	— John
Bar	— Baruch	1 Jn	— 1 John
1 Chr	— 1 Chronicles	2 Jn	— 2 John
2 Chr	— 2 Chronicles	3 Jn	— 3 John
Col	— Colossians	Jon	— Jonah
1 Cor	— 1 Corinthians	Jos	— Joshua
2 Cor	— 2 Corinthians	Jude	— Jude
Dn	— Daniel	1 Kgs	— 1 Kings
Dt	— Deuteronomy	2 Kgs	— 2 Kings
Eccl	— Ecclesiastes	Lam	— Lamentations
Eph	— Ephesians	Lk	— Luke
Est	— Esther	Lv	— Leviticus
Ex	— Exodus	Mal	— Malachi
Ez	— Ezekiel	1 Mc	— 1 Maccabees
Ezr	— Ezra	2 Mc	— 2 Maccabees
Gal	— Galatians	Mi	— Micah
Gn	— Genesis	Mk	— Mark
Hb	— Habakkuk	Mt	— Matthew
Heb	— Hebrews	Na	— Nahum
Hg	— Haggai	Neh	— Nehemiah
Hos	— Hosea	Nm	— Numbers
Is	— Isaiah	Ob	— Obadiah
Jas	— James	Phil	— Philippians
Jb	— Job	Phlm	— Philemon
Jdt	— Judith	Prv	— Proverbs
Jer	— Jeremiah	Ps(s)	— Psalms
Jgs	— Judges	1 Pt	— 1 Peter
		2 Pt	— 2 Peter

Rom	— Romans	1 Thes	— 1 Thessalonians
Ru	— Ruth	2 Thes	— 2 Thessalonians
Rv	— Revelation	Ti	— Titus
Sir	— Sirach	1 Tm	— 1 Timothy
1 Sm	— 1 Samuel	2 Tm	— 2 Timothy
2 Sm	— 2 Samuel	Wis	— Wisdom
Song	— Song of Songs	Zec	— Zechariah
Tb	— Tobit	Zep	— Zephaniah

OTHER ABBREVIATIONS

DM	Dives in Misericordia	OR	Osservatore Romano
FC	Familiaris Consortio	RH	Redemptor Hominis
GS	Gaudium et Spes	SC	Sacrosanctum Concilium
LG	Lumen Gentium		
MC	Marialis Cultus	SD	Salvifici Doloris

INDEX AND REFERENCES

SEASON OF ADVENT

SEASON OF CHRISTMAS

Help us to live the Gospel with the "folly" of the Cross: OR 19 (5-8-84).

SEASON OF EASTER

140 Teach us the attitudes of the Good Shepherd: OR 17 (4-27-82). **141** Beloved Daughter of the Father: OR 26 (6-26-84). **141** The salvific will of God: OR 26 (6-26-84). **142** A Mother's right: OR 19 (5-8-79). **142** All-powerful intercession: OR 19 (5-8-79). **143** A Motherly presence: OR 19 (5-8-79). **144** The fulfillment of the salvific mystery: OR 19 (5-8-79). **144** Bringing young people to Mary: OR 19 (5-8-79). **145** The fullest expression of fidelity to the Spirit: OR 19 (5-8-79). **145** The understanding of mysteries: OR 15 (4-12-83). **146** Cause of our joy: OR 15 (4-12-83). **146** Queen of Heaven: OR 15 (4-12-83). **147** The most precious fruit: OR 16 (4-19-83). **147** Most exalted "accomplishment" of the Paschal Mystery: OR 16 (4-9-83). **148** Following Mary's example: OR 16 (4-9-83). **149** The mercy of Mary: DM 9. **150** Mary's participation in the revelation of mercy: DM 9. **150** A profound knowledge of the Divine Mercy: DM 9. **151** Learning to love: DM 9. **152** The gifts that assure our eternal salvation: DM 9. **153** Mother of the Church: RH 22. **154** The grace of Divine Motherhood: RH 22. **155** The Church looks to Mary with hope: RH 22. **155** Mother of Consolation: OR 17 (4-22-80). **156** Mary strengthens our faith: OR 17 (4-22-80). **156** Loving consolatrix: OR 17 (4-22-80). **157** The mission of the Virgin in the plan of salvation: OR 17 (4-26-83). **158** She lives with the Lord: OR 17 (4-26-83). **159** Extraordinary guide: OR 24 (6-12-84). **159** Mother of Christ the Liberator: OR 24 (6-12-84). **160** Strengthen your drooping hands: OR 24 (6-12-84). **160** The blessedness of faith: OR 25 (6-19-79). **161** "Anyone who does not take up the cross . . .": OR 25 (6-19-79). **162** "All ages to come shall call me blessed": OR 25 (6-19-79). **162** Disinterested love: OR 25 (6-19-79). **163** "Whoever loves God . . .": OR 25 (6-19-79). **163** Eager in her joy: OR 25 (6-19-79). **164** Joyful in hope: OR 25 (6-19-79). **164** Your fruit is blessed: OR 38 (9-18-84). **165** The Mother of the Lord comes: OR 38 (9-18-84). **166** She believed in this mystery: OR 38 (9-18-84). **166** The faith of Mary: OR 38 (9-18-84).

ORDINARY TIME

Printed: **t.s.g.** - Asti